Teaching the Monkey to *fly*

A Step by Step Guide to Self-Empowerment

By

Jann Weiss

Published by:

Kima Global Publishers,
P.O. Box 374,
Rondebosch,
7701
Cape Town
South Africa

First Edition April 1999

Weiss Transformation Tape sets; *e*-mail to **kima@gem.co.za**

Comments and feedback to: **helpufly@global.co.za**

ISBN 0-9584065-6-1

Dedication

To the growing family of courageous Humans who are waking up and becoming Human Souls. You are not alone. We can do this. We **are** doing this.

Acknowledgments

Thank you…to all the hearts whose love and support helped to create this work. Thanks to my Publisher, Robin in South Africa, for his beyond the call of duty patience. Thanks to Patricia in Italy for the laptop upon which this was written. Thanks to all the loving, caring friends on three continents who encouraged, carried, fed, shared their homes, and prodded me through the two-year long project. Your faces are in front of me now. I thank you and I love you too.

To all the Unseen Beings who have guided and inspired me, I telepathically project a huge thanks. And to all of you who have been asking "When's the book coming out?", verily I say unto thee "Soon has finally happened."

Contents

Introduction

Teaching The Monkey To Fly is the result of 15 years of working with people whose lives are dedicated to their spiritual development and evolution. It is also being written in response to the overwhelming demand from those same people that I "write it all down".

The processes taught in this book are the result of higher guidance and inspiration being applied to my own personal healing work. They have proved successful not only for myself but also for hundreds of thousands of others as I have shared them around the world. It wasn't my plan to be sharing something that was, for me, so personal. When people close to me saw me change, and asked that they be shown what I was doing, however, I complied. When I saw *their* results, I began including these processes in the self-improvement workshops that were already a part of my work. Soon I was being asked to show others how to teach The Processes and the Facilitator Trainings began. The Living In Truth Institute came into existence at that same time in order to support our new facilitators.

We now have a worldwide network of people who have come together using The Weiss Transformation Processes. In places like North and South America, Europe and South Africa, individuals with the courage to move beyond limitations and set-in-stone belief systems are taking their lives back. They are learning to love and empower themselves in a way that results in a reality of less fear and struggle and more peace and freedom. They are creating miracles.

This book is about *your* ability to create miracles in your life. It will address the quality of your life. You will be given the opportunity to identify what drives you and creates your responses to the people and experiences around you. You will be introduced to specific techniques that will enable you to modify or eliminate what isn't working for you and to amplify what is working for you. It is a step-by-step guide for self-empowerment and in addition to the in-depth explanations of the concepts behind the processes, will also include your own personal work in the form of "Doing Pages", "Homework" and "Summary Sheets". You will be asked to log and record your information and experiences as you go so that the results of your efforts will be clearer to you. All of this is designed to support you in getting the most out of this guide to *your* personal empowerment.

A magical story has been woven throughout the book, reflecting our struggle for greater expression and is included to create an understanding of the larger ramifications of individual efforts. I also wanted to add something to the book purely for the fun of it. I believe that "fun" is important too.

Now, in response to all those folks who have been requesting that I "write it all down", I give them and you *Teaching The Monkey To Fly; A Step by Step Guide to Self-empowerment"*.

* * *

As each of us increases the amount of love within,
the amount of love in the world is increased
by that same amount.

As each of us decreases the amount of fear within
the amount of fear in the world is decreased
by that same amount.

One way or the other
we have an effect on our species
and on our world.

THE STORY

Part One

If only I could Fly

If Only I Could Fly

*H*e *stands at the edge of the jungle that is his Home. He looks out into the Open Space that he is forbidden to explore. He is the oldest of the Young Ones and he knows that he can get into trouble for staying too long here at The Edge. How can the others not want to know what's out there? How can they not want to explore that incredibly large inviting world beyond the trees? There are, after all, more of us Two-Leggeds than Four-Leggeds.*

He's heard the stories. He's heard how the Four-Leggeds can grab you up and make you their meal. He's been told that in the jungle, when Four-Leggeds come looking for their meal, having trees to run up into is the only thing that keeps his people from being eaten. 'Trees are our food, home and safety." How many times has he heard that?

A small rustle of leaves behind him tells him he's not alone. He turns, afraid that he's in trouble one more time. Three small faces peering out from the bushes tell him otherwise and he relaxes. It's just some of the other Young Ones. They won't come out from the bushes to speak to him; he's too near The Edge and they know the stories as well as he does.

He speaks to them anyway, "You don't have to be afraid. It's really quite safe here and look, I'm not being hurt." They stare at him with fear in their eyes as he turns back toward the Open Space. "One day I'm going to find out what's out there." The sudden rustle of leaves tells him that he's once again alone.

After a little while, he sighs and turns to go back. As he turns he sees The Eldest One sitting watching him. He knows very well that The Eldest One is to be obeyed and feared. Instead of rushing forward to herd him back with smacks and blows as the Elders usually did, The Eldest One drew closer and began to speak.

"To go there is to die", he said. "Others have gone and have never returned, except for a few. Those few who did return were crazy and spoke of such things as places of land higher than our Trees and water larger in size than our Home. We know that these things are not true. If they were, we would be

able to see them from our Lookout Tree which we all know is the very tallest place in the world."

The Eldest One looked troubled for a moment and then continued. "The stories of high land and large water caused great confusion among our people. Some became very afraid and began running in circles screaming at the storyteller. Others wanted to leave our Home to find these places. The confusion and arguing was great and upset every one of our people. So the crazy one was killed and peace was restored. So you see, Young One, to go there *is* to die. Life in the trees is safe. Return with me now."

It was important to obey The Eldest One and life in the trees **was** safe, so he went back into the jungle as he was told. However, whenever he was sure he was unobserved by the Elders, he returned to The Edge. He thought about land higher than the trees and a place with large water.

He was aware that from time to time other Young Ones stood behind him in the bushes. He would talk to them repeating "You don't have to be afraid. It's really quite safe here and look, I'm not being hurt." None would stand with

7

him at The Edge, but they sometimes kept him company from the bushes just the same.

One day he decided he wanted to know more about the size of his Home so he went to the Lookout Tree. He began to work his way to the top and was about half way up when he was stopped by a Lookout Elder who told him "You must not be here."

"I've come to Learn", he replied as boldly as he could.

After a very long moment the Elder nodded and accompanied him to the top, where what he saw nearly caused him to lose his grip on the branch. He saw... His Home... spreading out for as far as he could see, until it touched the sky in three directions. In the other direction the treeless Open Space went on until it ended at the Sky.

He looked hard out into the Open Space for any sign of tall land or large water. He saw only grass and small bushes. He continued to look hard as the Elder watched him closely. "As you can clearly see", said the Elder, "our Home is larger than anything else except the Sky." He nodded at the Elder, disappointed.

8

Suddenly he saw something in the grass moving toward the trees.

"What is that?" he asked. The Elder's response almost cost him his grip on the branch for a second time. The Elder began jumping and screaming "Four-Legged, a Four-Legged is coming into our Home" and he flew down the tree barely touching the branches in an effort to warn the others.

This left the oldest of the Young Ones alone at the top of Lookout Tree. He could hear the screams and cries of the others as they made their way up into the safety of the jungle's trees. He could see the Four Legged as it continued to make it's way into his Home.

He was surprised at how calm he was. The presence of a Four-Legged was a dangerous thing and usually quite upsetting for him. Perhaps it was because he was so far above all of the frantic activity. Perhaps it was because of the new perspective this height gave him. He wasn't sure. He only knew that something profound had changed in him. He also knew that one day he would find a way to experience what was in that place where the Open Space ended and the Sky began. One day he would find a way. If only he could fly...

CHAPTER ONE

Monkeys <u>Cannot</u> Fly

We live on a planet of nearly six billion fairly intelligent human beings; a planet that could be perceived as a garden. For the most part, our species seems oblivious to this fact as we busy ourselves with the struggle for survival. The opportunity to experience and enjoy what this planet has to offer is here for us all. Few of us have the time, the energy or the inclination, however, to truly comprehend the remarkable place in which we live.

We do not appreciate the incredible garden around us because we do not appreciate (or even know about) the incredible garden within. We have no idea of what we truly are and what we are truly capable of creating. We look out at the world through the eyes of a body that is limited in its capacity to perceive. We look at ourselves through perspectives and beliefs that are limited and one-sided.

Our perspective and our life's experiences are the result of stored information that is both *genetic* (inherent within the body) and *cultural* (learned) in origin. This information shapes our responses to the outside world. It also dictates how much or how little we contribute to that world as well as how that contribution will look. It is important to understand that *everything* your body does is the result of stored information. This information is electro-chemical in nature. Understanding this is the first step to finding the power to change not only your body's responses, but to finding your ability to consciously create your reality; your life.

Human DNA primarily contains survival information (as

much as 95%). I call this our Primate Survival Information because our bodies share this same genetic information with the bodies of chimps and gorillas. This is not to say that **we** are the same as chimps and gorillas, only that our bodies share a great deal of the same stored information and therefore, a great many of our automatic responses are the same. (This subject will be discussed in much greater detail in the following chapters.) This genetic data tells our bodies how to react to potentially threatening situations; what is commonly referred to as "fight or flight" behavior. It is this information that also allows us the reality of fear, anger, rage and hate; and as a matter of survival, also allows us compassion and love.

It is interesting that, for our bodies, both anger and love are deemed necessary for survival. Anger, used to compensate for another primate response called fear, is also employed as an automatic response to aggression on the part of another. Love (and compassion) on the other hand, are necessary to ensure cooperation between species members and is used in support of the young.

Our bodies begin accumulating cultural information as soon they are conceived. Because the mother's emotional reactions are a chemical phenomenon the baby is physically influenced by her emotional reactions and responses. The baby also learns the mother's responses through the medium of sound. It will be influenced by her chemical reaction to the sound that is Dad, or Grandma, or men and women's voices in general. The baby's body learns what sounds cause fear, what sounds cause tension and what sounds result in peace or lack of tension through the mother's responses.

The birthing process is another experience in which the baby's body accumulates large and important amounts of information. Though there is rarely a conscious memory of this experience, as the child grows older the *body* remembers for as long as the memory (information) is stored. How the baby is handled, the kinds of sounds it hears, how often the sounds are reassuring, how often the sounds are detached and clinical; all this begins giving the baby information about how safe it is in this new "outside of mom" place.

As the child continues to grow so does the accumulation of information. The education expands to include information concerning communication and behavior modification; learning how and when to get ideas across and which behavior is acceptable or not acceptable. Equally as important is the education that a child begins receiving about its self-worth. It is this stored information that we will most often be addressing in this work.

A child decides its value or self-worth as a direct result of how it sees itself being treated and perceived by the other important individuals in its environment; those individuals involved with its survival. If a parent acts as though the child is precious and valuable, then the child will accept this as truth and treat itself and others accordingly. If the parent, however, mixes this feedback with an understanding that the child is only precious when it's engaging in acceptable behavior, then the child becomes confused, frustrated and eventually angry. If a parent acts as though the child is a nuisance or something less than valuable, then the child will accept this as truth and treat itself and others accordingly.

There is an interesting thing that happens in the human psyche when it's confronted with negative self-value feedback and this has to do with the nature of our basic genetic information. The majority of our genetic data is about staying alive i.e. avoiding death. ***This is the body's number one priority.*** As a result of this, the body is constantly on guard against any and all potential threats. The body equates all negativity as something to be on guard against; all negativity is considered a threat. Therefore, negative feedback has a greater effect on the individual than does positive feedback. This is why a child given both positive and negative self-worth feedback will notice, ***remember*** and respond more frequently to the negative feedback. It's an unconscious survival response. This is also why giving repetitive positive feedback is so important; to insure that the child remembers and stores this information adequately.

As we look around our planet and observe how humans are treating each other it's very easy to see the kind of information that has been stored in most human bodies. Survival motivated behavior is the easiest to see in our species. Any conflict dealing with territory is motivated by a primate response; whether it's a country or a parking place that's being fought over. Another example of primate motivated behavior is greed. The unconscious need to have enough of whatever it takes to survive causes many to engage in unkind and insensitive behavior.

Conflicts over the issue of power can be both genetic and cultural in their origin. If the individual is responding to an underlying negative self-value, then they may compensate for this by causing others to appear more negative. Pecking order behavior among children and adults is a perfect example of culturally motivated power issues.

The genetic motivation for power conflicts is the individual's unconscious desire not to die. Someone else having too much power may result in the individual being hurt, either physically or emotionally. (Keep in mind that the words *hurt* and *death* have equal value to the body.) If a flight response isn't acceptable for the individual then the potential threat must be compensated for. Most often this is done by posturing, raising the voice, the use of anger and sometimes with the use of violence.

It is the body's primate survival responses causing the majority of the violence and upheaval on our planet today. From phobias and drug addictions to road rage and rape; all are the response to a combination of genetic survival information and negative self-value information influencing the body.

Most religions were meant to off-set the negative primate responses and encourage the positive ones of love and compassion. Instead, they've become one more excuse for angry and aggressive behavior. Abortion clinic bombings, the Catholic-Protestant Irish conflict and the chaos of the Middle East are a few examples. Though most of these are also about the loss or gain of territory, religion is the main excuse used for killing one another. This is not to say that every member of our species is using religion as a reason for conflict, only that for the most part, this is what it has become on our planet.

If the primate survival perspective is the predominant motivational force in us, then territorial disputes, wars and fighting over wealth or food can only increase as our population grows. Indeed, as we look around the planet, it appears as though this is already happening. Does this mean that our species is doomed to eventually exterminating itself?

How then, do we get beyond the fear, the aggression, the primate in us? Every day brings us examples of just how difficult it is to overcome or suppress these behaviors. Not smoking that next cigarette; not eating that next tasty but unhealthy bit of food; not screaming at a child because you're at your wits end; not worrying about the too small numbers showing up in your checkbook; not taking that next drink that will make it all better; how easy or difficult are all these things?

Not responding with anger when someone insults you, not closing off when your criticized, not redefining the person who just cut you off in traffic as a very small portion of the anatomy; how common are these things? How frequently, how often, how completely are anger, frustration and fear a part of our thought processes and responses? Lately, world and religious leaders have spent a lot of time apologizing for their inability to resist or suppress their human nature.

For the most part we seem powerless over these things. Prayer and meditation can take us out of it for a little while, but the basic responses are still within us and overcoming them ourselves? Must it be a matter of mind *over* matter? Is there another less stressful and more loving way to co-exist with our bodies? ...or are we after all, *only* human?

Summary

The Body's Perspective

DNA INFORMATION Genetic	+	CULTURAL INFORMATION Learned	=	OUR REALITY
SURVIVAL BEHAVIOR Fight or Flight	+	SELF WORTH (Positive self value feedback & Negative self value feedback)	=	RESPONSES TO LIFE Combination self value
SURVIVAL BEHAVIOR (I am valuable and equal to others)	+	POSITIVE FEEDBACK	=	FULFILMENT (Relationships display cooperation & love)
SURVIVAL BEHAVIOR (I am not valuable and equal to others)	+	NEGATIVE FEEDBACK	=	AGRESSION (Relationships display separation & anger)
SURVIVAL BEHAVIOR (I am sometimes valuable and equal to others)	+	COMBINATION FEEDBACK	=	FEAR & STRESS (Relationships display competition & neediness)

Examples Of Genetic Information

Note: Our Genetic programming is an unconscious motivating force. As we discuss this subject, we are noting your *body's* responses. They will not usually reflect what you consciously think or believe.

1. Maintaining one's life force (keeping the body alive) is the primary goal.

2. The death of the body is the end to it's awareness, therefore death is the annihilation of Self.

Examples of every-day behavior and responses resulting from these first two underlying genetic realities are:

➢ Fear of the unknown – an "unknown" could be a threat, i.e. possible death.

➢ Fear of the dark – the dark holds "unknowns".

➢ Being startled by sudden noises – until the source of the noise is identified, it is an unknown – the louder and closer the noise, the greater the potential threat.

➢ Tension or nervousness around strangers – strangers are an "unknown".

➢ Tension (fear) in new situations or places – "new" means "unknown".

➢ Resistance to change – change can result in a "new" situation or make a change.

➢ Staying in a negative situation when logic indicates the need to make a change.

➢ The use of anger to compensate for fear makes it feel smaller than fear – anger is our body's way of "puffing up" when fear has made it feel smaller than the perceived threat.

➢ "Posturing" in new situations or around strangers.

➤ Physical or emotional withdrawal – used when anger or posturing are considered insufficient in compensating for a consciously or unconsciously perceived threat.

➤ Procurement of food, shelter and clothing – whether the individual creates these things for themselves, works in order to purchase these things from others or steals from others, the purpose is the same; to keep the individual alive.

3. Maintaining the continuity of the species is a secondary goal and has nearly the same importance as the primary goal.

Examples:

➤ Adultery and infidelity.

➤ The enthusiasm that most humans have for sex.

4. Determines how the body will physically look and function.

Examples:

➤ Features, build and skin tone.

➤ Propensity for certain diseases and ailments.

Examples Of Cultural Information

Note: Cultural programming varies from place to place around our planet. This treatment of the subject holds no judgment, it only notes the various forms of information that is passed on from adults to children.

1. Modifies the individual's genetic survival behavior in order to conform to and therefore not threaten the survival needs of the collective. The collective can be family, community, country or any other human grouping that the individual aligns with.

Examples:

➢ Waiting for your turn.

➢ Speaking when you're spoken to.

➢ Sharing the positive aspects of yourself.

➢ Not sharing the negative aspects of yourself.

➢ Not using violence on other members of your collective.

➢ Using your energy and time for the good of all.

➢ Charity.

➢ Not bringing "disgrace" to the collective.

2. Defines the individual's expected role or contribution within various collectives.

Examples:

➢ Statements such as "make us proud" or "don't let us down."

➢ Using gender to determine what an individual can and cannot do with her/his life.

➢ Using skin color to determine what an individual can or cannot do with his/her life.

➢ Carrying on family work ethics and traditions.

➢ Statements such as "behave yourself like a minister's son."

3. Defines the individual's Self Worth.

Examples:

➢ Being described as "being good" because of behavior that is deemed to be good.

➢ Being described as "being bad" because of behavior that is deemed to be bad.

➢ Receiving positive feedback for being smarter, faster and/or more productive.

➢ Receiving negative feedback for being dumber, slower and/or less productive.

➢ Receiving negative feedback for not being like others who represent the majority of the collective.

➢ Statements such as "why aren't you as smart as your sister/brother?" or "you'll never amount to anything, you're so stupid."

➢ Statements such as "I love you no matter what."

4. Defines the individual's relationship and behavior with members of the collective who have either a greater or lesser worth (power or authority).

Examples:

➢ Which tone of voice to use and when.

➢ Using or not using direct eye contact.

➢ Using or not using words such "please" and "thank you"

➢ Saluting, bowing, kneeling.

➢ Responses to various forms of uniforms (military, medical, religious etc.)

➤ Receiving aggressive behavior only from those who are greater in stature or identified as having greater power (parents, older siblings, teachers etc.)

Doing Pages

Getting To Know What's Influencing You

Using a separate sheet of paper and taking your time, record as honestly as you can your answers to the questions below. This is not a test. There are no right or wrong answers. This is simply an opportunity for you to know more about you.

Genetic Influences

1   Are you sometimes frustrated by your automatic responses to other people's behavior? Yes or no.

2   If yes, how often?   In a week?   In a day?   In an hour?

3   Are their any substances (certain foods, drugs or alcohol) that you sometimes just can't say "no" to?

4   If yes, list 2 of the substances and note specifically **when** you can't say "no".

Note: Don't forget things like pain killers and prescriptions.

5   List 3 of your strongest negative emotional responses and exactly what triggers them.

6   List 3 of your strongest positive emotional responses and exactly what triggers them.

7   How would your life be different if you could truthfully answer "no" to Question 3?

8   Would your life be different if you truthfully didn't have any response to Question 5?

9   List 3 re-occurring automatic fear responses over which you have no control.

Cultural Influences

1   As a child, most people received both positive and negative self-value feedback. What kind of feedback do you most remember? positive or negative?

2   List 5 examples of *verbal* positive self-value feedback that you remember receiving as a child.

3   List 5 examples of *non-verbal* positive self-value feedback that you remember receiving as a child.

4   List 5 examples of *verbal* negative self-value feedback that you remember receiving as a child.

5   List 5 examples of *non-verbal* negative self-value feedback that you remember receiving as a child.

6   Record your first remembered "good boy" or "good girl" feedback.

7   Record your first remembered "bad girl" or "bad boy" feedback.

8   Do you worry about what others think of you? yes or no.

Note: The answer "sometimes" is the same as "yes"

9   Do you truly believe that you are a good person?

10 Do you believe that you could be better?

11 Do you believe that you are a work in progress?

12 Is there any difference in your mind between Questions 10 and 11?

Home Work Page

Noticing What's Influencing You

The Homework Pages are designed to create the opportunity for you to discover how this chapter's information might apply in your life. It's also to support you in becoming more consciously aware of exactly how your body's programming is affecting your daily behavior and reactions.

Your Daily Behavior Log should include 3 or more situations (positive or negative) that occurred during the day.

1 Briefly record the situation.

2 List as many of the responses and reactions to the situation as you can observe in yourself.

3 Determine whether each response or reaction was motivated by genetic or cultural programming (or both) and note the reasons why.

You can record your self-observations as you go through your day or you can record them in the evening before going to bed. Again, this is not a test and there are no right or wrong

answers. This is simply an opportunity for you to know more about you.

After a week of logging three situations a day, you will find that you will begin to automatically determine the origin of your reactions and behavior as you go through your day. At this point you can discontinue keeping your Log or you can continue recording, just for the fun of it. Either way, you are now much more aware of "what's influencing you".

The following is an example of a possible Log entry:

MY DAILY BEHAVIOR LOG

Nov. 03, Thursday

Situation: I walked by a homeless person.

Reaction 1:   I found myself walking quickly past him.

Reaction 2:   I looked away, I couldn't look at him.

Reaction 3:   I noticed tension in my body, I was afraid of him.

Reaction 4:   For the next half hour I was impatient and angry with everyone.

Notes on Reaction 1

I wanted to get away from him as quickly as possible.

"Getting away quickly " = I was afraid = "flight" behavior.

Therefore walking quickly away = **genetic** fear response.

Notes on Reaction 2

I looked away because I didn't want to have to interact with him.

"Didn't want to have to interact" = I was afraid = "flight" behavior.

Therefore, looking away = **genetic** fear response.

I looked away because I was embarrassed for him.

"Embarrassed for him" = I remember many times seeing my father being embarrassed if we didn't have enough money for something or couldn't afford things like my Grandfather could. and

"Embarrassed for him" = I remember my mother yelling at me once when I came home very, very dirty from school "do you want people to think you're poor, stupid and lazy? What will people think of your father and I?"

Therefore, looking away = **cultural** programming

Notes on Reaction 3

I noticed tension in my body, I was afraid of him

I guess I thought he might hurt me = something unknown might hurt me.

Therefore, the unknown = fear = **genetic** programming

Notes on Reaction 4

I was impatient with everyone because I was angry at myself for my reaction to him.

I felt stupid. When I feel stupid, I feel small. When I feel small, I sometimes take it out on other people = pecking order behavior.

Therefore, taking it out on other people = **genetic** response

Summary for Situation #1

I walked by a homeless person today and I observed myself responding with my body's primate "flight" and "pecking order" responses.

I walked by a homeless person today and I observed myself responding with responses that I learned from my parents during my childhood.

CHAPTER TWO

and I'm Not A Monkey

I am a Soul struggling to remember that fact while under the influence of Being Human

This statement, more than any, seems to sum up our experience on this planet. We are not monkeys, but genetically speaking, our bodies are and the body's influence does frequently seem insurmountable. The good news, however, is we are not the body; we are what lives in it. We aren't the physical form that we walk around in, we are something much, much more. In this work, it will be referred to as the Soul or the Higher Self. It is who and what we actually are.

The definition of Soul that we will be using here is; that aspect of Self that connects us to the Godhead, Source or Creator (use whichever terminology works for you). It is also seen as that aspect of the Godhead, Source or Creator flowing through and animating our human form.

This means that we have direct access to a part of ourselves that has a perspective based on love, compassion, wisdom and peace. It means that we can access a reality that does not include fear, self-judgment, struggle or hate. It also means that we can tap into our Soul's awesome creative power.

It's not enough to read about or intellectually understand the Soul's principles of love and non-judgment. Being well versed doesn't change *our body's* inherent fear and survival responses. It's not enough to occasionally, or even frequently, visit those states of mind that allow us to experience the Soul's reality of love and non-judgment. This only gives us a temporary break from those inherent fear and survival responses.

If we are going to change how our body behaves then we must change what our body believes. We must change the information upon which the behavior is based. The most efficient way of doing this is not just by opening to your source of higher perspective but by *integrating* your source of higher perspective with our body.

Imagine a huge reservoir of All-Knowing Mind pouring itself down through a very long funnel. Imagine that this funnel is connected to the head of a human being. The All-Knowing Mind pouring itself through the funnel is God, the Source or Creator. The very long funnel is The Soul or Higher Self.

Imagine that every human being has one of these funnel's connected to it's head. Look closely at the place where the funnel connects to the head. You will see that only the slightest of trickles of the Soul actually makes it's way into the body. Usually, it's just enough to animate the body. If you continue to watch you will see that occasionally the trickle is increased a little to add a bit more influence in the body. Interestingly, when this happens the human being calls the trickle "a still, small voice" or it's "conscience". Few human beings know about their connection (Soul) and that it can be experienced much more intimately or are aware of the benefits of doing so.

Praying is one of the ways of increasing the trickle. Sometimes you can see a human being going into a state of mind called "meditation". When they do this they are projecting their awareness up into the funnel exploring the Soul contained there. While they are doing this, more of the Soul leaks into the body. When this happens the body relaxes, the brain ceases its survival-related thinking and begins some degree of contemplation of the Stuff contained in the funnel.

This is a nice activity for the body and occasionally it enjoys it so much that it will go into a state of bliss.

After awhile, however, the human being must withdraw it's focus from the Stuff in the funnel and bring it's awareness back into the body in order to deal with the very real and practical daily matters of living. Eventually, the body's survival-related thinking will again take over. For most people, the effects of meditation and prayer don't seem to last very long before the body's primate genetic survival programming is once more in control.

These little vacations from stressful survival thinking are healthy and healing for the body and the increased flow of the Soul into the body is certainly a plus. Increasing this flow creates a greater understanding of life's circumstances and problems. When the trickle is increased to become even the smallest of flows, the experiences of love, peace, forgiveness, gratitude and inspiration are experienced in many more moments.

When the flow of Soul awareness becomes an ongoing conscious experience, the body's way of perceiving and responding is altered. The fearful responses are diminished and the peaceful, empowered responses are increased. Life's challenges become life's experiences and opportunities. The negativity of others becomes the creativity of others. Illness and fatigue, depression and loneliness become things of the past. Can you imagine waking each morning with a resounding "yes" and immense gratitude for yet another day in which to explore your self and your world? Well, that's how it is for a Soul who has been given the freedom to express itself completely through a human form.

The processes of meditation and prayer are seen as two very important ways of opening to the Soul's higher reality of love and joy. In this work, however, we will be exploring a third approach that can be used in addition to whatever spiritual or religious practices are currently being employed.

This new approach enhances and creates a more intimate relationship with whatever Higher Power the individual is aligned. This "more intimate relationship" is achieved not by praying to or going to a Higher Power that is outside ourselves. It's created by bringing that Higher Power directly into the body and integrating *what it knows* on a cellular, even genetic, level.

Heaven *on Earth* is what most of us desire (using Christian terminology).Visiting Heaven, though delightful and educational, isn't the answer. This still leaves Earth as a place full of inspired but struggling humans. The struggling humans must become more Heaven-like within themselves. The reality of Heaven must become part of the body's consciousness. In this way, our Earth can become a peaceful, supportive and truly joyful place in which to live no matter how many billions of humans play upon her surface.

We, the Being living in the body, know how to fly. Meditation, prayer and out-of-body experiences allow us to do this, creating the mental opportunities to explore other realms, other ways of being. Our bodies, however, know of no such freedom. They exist in and are limited to a time and gravity based reality. Physical exceptions to this are rare and deemed mystical or miracles.

There is a natural way to teach our monkey to fly; a way to physically step our body outside the limits of time and gravity. It can be done in a way that allows us to continue our functional day-to-day experiences and relationships without having to join a monastery or a new religion. The only things sacrificed are fear, doubt and self-judgment. The only investment required is time and intention. It's not magical, though it may feel that way from time to time. It's not mystical though it certainly is spiritual. It's not a trick, it's actually based on the very real laws of physics. Monkeys *can* fly... if you just know how to change the part of them which thinks they can't.

Summary

The Soul

➤ Is our connection to The Source.

➤ Is that aspect of The Source animating the human body.

➤ Is eternal.

➤ Exists in a reality that does not include primate survival perspectives.

➤ Exists in a reality that does include love and peace.

➤ Has an understanding of the greater purpose of everything.

➤ Understands the oneness and connectedness of all events and individuals.

➤ Cannot judge.

➤ Remains exclusively focused on the human body that it's animating.

➤ Is a constant source of higher perspective and inspiration.

Doing Pages

Getting To Know What's Influencing You

Soul Influences

Using a separate sheet of paper and taking your time, record as honestly as you can your answers to the questions below. (There are no right or wrong answers. This is simply an opportunity for you to know more about you.)

1. Has there ever been a time of extreme fear or distress when a sense of calm suddenly flowed through you?

2. If yes, to what do you attribute the sudden calm?

3. Have you ever been overwhelmed and in a state of confusion or indecision when you suddenly experienced incredible clarity and knew exactly what to do?

4. If yes, to what do you attribute the sudden clarity and knowingness?

5. Have you ever experienced moments of being much more than a human?

6. If yes, when was this?

7. Do you pray or meditate?

8. If yes, how often? In a week? In a day? In an hour?

9. If yes, do you feel more relaxed or peaceful after prayer or meditation?

10. If yes, for how long?

11. Do you think that your Soul (or Higher Power) has a fundamentally different perspective than you?

12. If yes, what do you think would be the biggest difference in your perspectives?

13. Do you think that your Soul's (or Higher Power's) perspective could benefit you in your day-to-day living?

14. If yes, what do you think would be the biggest benefit?

15. Are there other benefits?

16. What do you think your Soul (or Higher Power) believes about you?

17. What is the one thing that you would really like to ask your Soul (or Higher Power)?

18. What is the one thing, do you think, that your Soul (or Higher Power) would really like you to know?

19. Do you consider your Soul (or Higher Power) to be a partner?

20. If yes, why?   If no, why?

21. Do you believe that your Soul (or Higher Power) could help diminish your body's use of negative emotions?

22. Why?

23. Do you believe that your Soul (or Higher Power) could help diminish your life's negative experiences?

24. Why?

25. Is there a difference in the way you and your Soul (or Higher Power) experience the word "Love"?

26. If yes, what is the difference?

27. Is there a difference in the way you and your Soul (or Higher Power) experience the word "Self"?

28. If yes, what is the difference?

Home Work Page

Exploring the Soul's Influence

The Home Work Page is designed to support you in becoming more consciously aware of exactly how your Soul might affect your daily behavior and reactions.

Home Work – Part One

Perform the following visualization once or twice a day for three days. This process will take just a few minutes and is designed to create for you a new level of communication between your Soul and your Body. The process is most effective if done in a sitting position.

Step 1. Visualize a stream of energy or consciousness flowing from The Source down to the top of your head. Imagine that this stream of energy or consciousness is your Soul, your Higher Power. Keep in mind that it is only your Soul or Higher Power that you are working with here.

Step 2. Experience a small amount of this consciousness entering in through the top of your head.

Step 3. Imagine that an even greater flow of your Soul is spreading out in a bubble around you. Take a moment to feel the bubble of Soul energy in the air around you.

Step 4. Breathe your Soul's energy and consciousness into your body, allowing it to gently, gently flow through bones, muscles, organs and tissues.

Step 5. Notice your body's reaction to your Soul as you continue to quietly breathe.

Step 6. After a few minutes, thank your body and your Soul for the experience and bring your awareness back into the room.

Record your observations as soon after your experience as possible, noting both your physical and mental reactions.

Note: If "visualization" is something that is difficult for you, using your "imagination" can also create the experience for you.

Home Work – Part Two

Perform the following process once a day for three days. This process will take just a few minutes and is designed to create another level of support between your Soul and your Body. The process is most effective if done in a sitting position.

Step 1. Visualize a stream of energy or consciousness flowing from The Source down to the top of your head. Imagine that this stream of energy or consciousness is your Soul, your Higher Power. Keep in mind that it is only your Soul or Higher Power that you are working with here.

Step 2. Experience a small amount of this consciousness entering in through the top of your head.

Step 3. Imagine that an even greater flow of your Soul is spreading out in a bubble around you. Take a moment to feel the bubble of Soul energy in the air around you.

Step 4. Ask your Soul to create its reality of the word "Love" in its bubble in the air around you.

Step 5. Breathe your Soul's energy of "Love" into your body, allowing it to gently, gently flow through bones, muscles, organs and tissues.

Step 6. Notice your body's reaction to your Soul's reality. as you continue to quietly breathe.

Step 7. After a few minutes, thank your body and your Soul for the experience and bring your awareness back into the room.

You may find that you want to continue using this process substituting the following words in Step 4: Self Love, Truth, Higher Purpose, Higher Power, Freedom, Peace. Repeat the process three times for each new "word" and continue to record your experiences and observations as you do so.

Note: These experiences may be very strong and obvious or they may be much subtler. Noting your body's reaction during the process will be an indication that your Soul's reality is indeed having an effect on your body and that the experience is real.

THE STORY

Part Two

Do I Need Wings to Fly?

Do I Need Wings to Fly?

*I*n the days and months that followed, he was allowed to spend as much time as he wanted in the upper branches of Lookout Tree. He was careful not to get in the way of the Lookout Elders and listened quietly as they spoke of the different kinds of Four-Leggeds that they could see from this the highest place in their Home. They taught him about the other creatures that lived in the Open Space. They taught him about the many different kinds of birds that he could see flying from place to place. They also taught him the differences between the Four-Leggeds that were dangerous and those that did not come into their Home to eat his people.

On more than one occasion, he was the first to spot danger as it was slowly making it's way toward their Home. More than once he heard the Lookout Elders discussing what they called his Far-vision. He was happy to be making a contribution, but he was happier that his Far-vision ensured him a place in the highest branches. It was exciting to know that he was seeing as far as any of his people had ever seen.

One morning he was about to start the climb up to his favorite place when The Eldest One stopped him with the words, "I've heard that you have been very helpful in keeping our Home safe Young One."

"Yes", he replied nervously, "I have been helping."

The Eldest One looked at him for a long time and then said, "Perhaps you are ready to become a Lookout Elder. What do you think of this?"

He couldn't believe his ears. He was about to begin jumping and running in excited circles but caught himself. He was being told that he was no longer being looked on as a Young One.   He was being looked on as an Elder. He controlled his excitement and answered as calmly as he could, "Yes, Eldest One, I too think I am ready".

The Eldest One began speaking slowly to indicate that he must pay close attention. "It is wise that you use your vision for the good of our people rather than for curiosity is it not? So much more can be seen from the Lookout Tree than from The Edge where you frighten Young Ones. You have Far-vision Young Elder, use it wisely. Your vision and your imagination will give you the answers you seek." With this, The Eldest One turned and quietly moved away leaving the new Lookout Elder to ponder his words.

*He enjoyed his new position over the next few months and took his responsibility seriously. Each day, he took his turn at the top of Lookout Tree watching for any potential danger to his people. One day he realized that he had begun doing something different. He realized that he was seeing the approach of the Four-Leggeds much sooner when his mind became slightly unfocused or when he was close to dozing. He called it his "looking without looking". His ability to do this gave his people much more time to climb to safety and there was a great deal less panic among them when **his** warning call went out.*

He was happy to be making a contribution that brought greater peace to his Home. He was happy that The Eldest was pleased with him, for more than once when he returned to the Jungle floor to mingle with the others The Eldest One would say to him, "You are using your Far-vision wisely Young Elder". What really made him happy, however, was that he was learning to improve his Far-vision, and often as he sat in the highest branches looking out to the place where the Open Space

41

ended and the Sky began, he wondered, do I need wings to fly?

CHAPTER THREE

Creating Wings–Part One

We cannot control our own behavior and experiences indeed control our own lives until we understand and learn how to re-create those automatic responses that have been so powerfully creating our lives for us

In the first chapter we discussed how powerful the body's primate programming can be. We also discussed the influence of learned cultural programming in shaping our responses to the world. In the second chapter we looked at the effect opening to "another source" of information and influence has on the body, whether the source is the Soul, God and/or those Beings who reflect the Soul. Now it's time to take the next step of *integrating* the Higher Perspective into the body.

Although our physical body lives in a reality of fear and struggle, the consciousness animating the body does not. The consciousness animating the body exists in a reality in which the body's survival perspectives simply do not exist. This animating consciousness, the Soul, isn't capable of experiencing fear or judgment. It isn't capable of comprehending anything other than love, peace and an honest appreciation and understanding for everything occurring in your life.

Let's look at the example of experiencing the anger of another being directed at you. Your body's primate interpretation of the situation is that the other may be a possible threat to its welfare. Your body's primate response will be to either flee from the situation or to overpower the other by becoming angrier and louder, hopefully forcing the other to flee the situation. The end result will be unconscious fear, anger and stress lasting long after the situation has ended. The fear and stress will also contribute to the body's aging process.

The Soul has a completely different way of perceiving and responding to negativity. The Soul isn't capable of comprehending anything as a potential threat because it experiences everything as ultimately being the same Stuff. Everything, therefore, is equal to it. It will experience the other not just as an angry individual, but as a precious expression of The Source. It will also see the other as a co-creator in a potential learning or service situation for your body's inhabitant (you).

If your body were capable of a Soul's response, it would act very differently in this situation. You would be in peace with the other's anger and therefore avoid your own responses of fear, anger and stress. You might quietly move away from the situation or you might employ verbal responses reflecting your perspective of non-judgment and peace.

The end result of this Soul/Body response would be the lack of negative emotions stressing and aging the body. It would also create an environment more conducive to supporting the other in healing the cause of their anger. And, as you will see in a later chapter, your ability to experience the other as a precious expression of The Source would support the other in healing the need to use anger. If a physical defense did become necessary, the body's actions would flow and look very much like a dance with the other person, although when living in the Soul's reality, situations requiring physical defense rarely occur.

Etheric Teachers, Guides, Saints, Angels and Masters share the same perspective of oneness as your Soul. These Higher

Beings exist as a source of inspiration and influence for those of us who are living in physical bodies. Christ and Buddha, for example, are two of these Masters who have given us very real examples of how to physically live the higher perspectives of love and non-judgment.

Most people on our planet have a belief that there are non-physical Beings who exist to support us, not just in matters of survival, but also in developing a greater understanding of who and why we are. Communication in one form or another with these Higher Beings is woven into nearly every culture. It's accepted that these Beings have either a power and/or a perspective that would prove beneficial to those who are open to it.

Opening to the greater wisdom of a Higher Being can indeed create greater wisdom for our mind. Integrating that Higher Mind's *way of being*, however, can create healing, peace and spiritual transformation for our body.

Imagine not having to pray for help in getting through a stressful or fearful situation because your body is full of Angelic peace. Imagine being able to respond to negative people with compassion because the prevailing energy in your body is love. Imagine looking at yourself in the mirror and seeing yourself with Christ's eyes. Imagine taking on any goal with the wisdom and power of your Soul. Imagine looking at the world's chaos and experiencing the peace an ascended Master might experience, knowing that the chaos is actually a form of transformation.

What would it be like if Higher Wisdom were the primary influence in your body instead of primate survival programming? The processes taught in this book are designed to support you in creating just that; a new primary influence for your body.

The first of the Weiss Transformation Processes (The WTP's) was developed in November of 1989 as the result of my Etheric Spiritual Teachers supporting me through the loss of a baby. During this healing process I was urged to include one of my Highest Teachers (Christ) in the experience of the grief and anger. This simple act of allowing the Teacher to feel the emotions **with me** created not only a release of the emotions, but a new perspective on the entire experience. The higher purpose for both myself and the baby's soul was now completely understood and accepted with peace.

When I expressed my gratitude to my Teachers for their wonderful support, I was urged to "go deeper and take your Teacher with you". What happened next changed my life forever. I began exploring a deeper level of anger and sense of loss; emotions that I recognized as "leftovers from my childhood". I'd experienced these feelings before during various forms of therapy employed over a 14-year period attempting to heal from an abusive childhood. This time, however, when I allowed my Teacher to feel the emotions with me, I was amazed at the results. This time the feelings seemed to dissolve and entirely new perspectives emerged in their place.

Each emotional memory turned into an insight. I learned to see with new eyes. I learned to see with Christ's eyes. For example, as a child I thought that it was hate that I'd seen in my mother's face when she was punishing me. I was sure that my mother hated me, why else would she treat her child that way? With my new vision, however, I could see that it was actually frustration that was her motivation. She didn't hate me; she hated her life.

As my Teacher and I continued to re-experience my childhood I made another very important discovery. My mother actually loved me. Though I didn't remember her showing it very often after the age of five, my new vision allowed me to see that in spite of her behavior my mother actually did love me. This was a very necessary piece of information for my overall healing.

After two months of applying my new vision to "every bad thing that I could remember happening to me", I found myself looking at my entire childhood differently. I also found myself looking at my entire life differently. I wasn't angry at everything any more. I had more patience with others and with myself (a minor miracle).

As I expressed my continuing gratitude to my Teachers for their incredible support, I was once more urged to "go deeper and take your Teacher with you". Thinking I'd already done a fairly decent amount of healing, I asked "why". "Exactly", they responded. "Go deeper, ask why". So I did, and what I saw next changed everything... again.

With my Teacher and my new vision, I looked at my life asking the important question; why. Why physical and sexual abuse in my childhood? Why alcoholism and drug abuse in my twenties. Why suicide attempts in my thirties? Why the long road of self healing through my thirties and forties? And why, through it all, did I have a powerful connection to Spirit and a psychic ability that always seemed to lead me to helping others with similar issues? Suddenly, it was as if a curtain parted and I "saw". Every bad thing that had ever happened to me was to teach me compassion. The steps that I would be taught in my own healing would be something that I would share with others.

My life's purpose was clear and acceptable to me for the first time. My life's traumas were clear and forgivable for the first time. My parents could be seen as Soul friends fulfilling an agreement. My Teachers became my partners and my new vision became a way of life.

Fourteen years of prayer, meditation, gestalt therapy, guided visualizations, re-birthing, and other forms of group therapy all served to create a greater understanding of my lower nature and higher support. It wasn't until I allowed the higher support to enter into my lower nature, however, that my real healing began and The Weiss Transformation Processes were born.

The WTP's are based on the understanding that when Higher Truth is introduced into the body's negativity, the negativity is neutralized and replaced with the Higher Truth. The same way that warm air can transform a solid block of ice into a fluid, Truth (and love) will alter hate (and fear).

There are two ways of explaining why this is so; one is a left-brain, physics approach and the other is a right-brain, spiritual approach. Let's begin with the left-brain approach and a brief discussion of the nature of thought. In terms of physics, thought can be seen as an expression of energy, just as light and sound are expressions of energy. As energy they have either a higher or lower frequency.

For example, if you think of a rainbow with all the colors sitting next to each other, it's easy to see the way light breaks down into its different frequencies. Colors are, after all, individual light frequencies; where red is a lower frequency than violet. A piano keyboard is a way of visualizing the individual frequencies of sound; where low C is a lower frequency than high C. Thought, though not as easy to visualize as rainbows and keyboards, is very much the same kind of phenomenon. The human experience of individual thought frequencies are the emotions where hate (especially self-hate) is a lower frequency than love.

When we correctly combine higher and lower frequencies of color together, a magical thing happens; new colors. When we correctly combine higher and lower frequencies of sound together, another magical thing happens; harmony. When we correctly combine higher and lower frequencies of thought together, a really magical thing happens; healing and personal transformation. Correctly combining the Soul's love with the body's fear will create a new reality for you and your body. This then, is the left-brain explanation of why the WTP's work. Now, let's explore the right-brain, spiritual approach.

We are not the body, we are what animates the body. What animates the body can be called "Soul". We are, therefore, a Soul animating a body. Soul only knows Truth. As a result of this, Soul's perspective is one of peace, compassion and love. Therefore, our true nature is one of peace, compassion and love. The tendency to forget all of this when focusing through the senses of a body doesn't change our true nature. It only changes our ability to express our true nature.

Some Souls primarily concern themselves with more completely understanding the concepts of darkness and evil. (These folks would probably never find themselves picking up this book.) Other Souls want to explore their ability to maintain their higher perspective while under the influence of the body's five senses. Still others want to know if it's possible to change the body in a way that will create the Soul's ability to express itself freely and completely. (It is for these Souls that the WTP's and this book were created.)

Because fear is not our nature, we have the power to change the fear in our body. Because anger and self-hate are not our nature, we have the power to change these perspectives as well. Because we are, in essence, the Allness Itself, we have the power to create the reality of our true nature in the physical, primate forms that we live in. This then, is the right-brain explanation of why the WTP's work.

All of the Processes employ the technique of focusing a Higher Perspective directly into the body's emotions or memories. The source of the Higher Perspective is different in each of the Processes. The first of the processes (The Basic Process), uses the Soul or a trusted Support Being as the source of the Higher Perspective. In WTP Two – The Time Process, a Future Self supplies the new perspective (Chapter 5). In WTP Three – The DNA Process, we work with specific dimensional Aspects of the Soul in order to create a new primate perspective (Chapter 7). Although each of the Processes is used to heal or transmute different types of information or perspective being held in the body, the goal is always the same; to create the reality of *your* higher Truth in your body.

In this chapter, we will be working with WTP One – The Basic Process. In this Process, the source of higher perspective can either be The Soul or a trusted Support Being. A trusted Support Being might be Christ, Buddha, an Angel or any Master or Teacher who you know exists in Truth and who you trust will make the effort to work with you in your healing.

It's important to be sure that your body trusts the Support Being as well. It's the *body's* perspectives that are being changed and altered. It's therefore important to make sure that the body is, after all, open to the Being you are choosing to work with you. As an example, often individuals will choose to work with God, stating that they intend to work only with the very highest. However, as they discuss this, their body can be seen to tense each time they mention the word "God". This is an indication that, though the individual trusts God, their body does not. For some bodies, "God" is just too big or too powerful, and opening to something that big actually creates a fear response. If your body is afraid of your choice, then it won't allow the openness necessary to create the partnership needed for the Process to work.

On the other hand, your body will also not respond to the Process if it does not sense enough power in the chosen Support Being. From time to time, I will hear someone express the wish to work with a deceased Mother or Grandmother who has become a kind of spiritual guide or teacher for them. In these cases, the body will relate to the Mother or Grandmother as though they were still physical (which is how it remembers them) and not as the more evolved Beings that they may have become.

If your desire is to simply work with your own Soul, be sure that your body has the same sense of it that you do and hasn't decided that, like God, it's a concept that's just too big.

When choosing the appropriate Support Being, notice your body's response when you focus on or think about the Being. If your body relaxes (sometimes with an audible exhale of the breath), it's an indication of trust. If it doesn't relax, then there's a good chance that it's not experiencing the Being the same way you do and you might want to shift your focus to another source of support.

Over the years, I have found that most bodies are amazingly trusting of Angels, even when the individual doesn't think they believe in them. Angels are Beings who have never been in physical form, have never experienced judgment or anger and who are not so frightening a thing to open to. For those for whom nothing else seems to work, opening to "the energy of Love" or "the energy of Truth" will often be the answer.

Take some time before starting the Process to determine exactly which source of support works for you and your body. Reconfirm your choice each time you begin to work because there will be occasions when you have either evolved to another level of work and need another level of assistance, or the issue you'll be working on may require a different kind of support.

It's important not to get too caught up in trying to do it exactly right, or in creating a fear that you might do it wrong. It's not really a matter of being able to do it wrong. No matter what you work with, some degree of healing or change will occur. The power of your Soul, combined with your intention to create a healing, plays a very large part in achieving your goal. Trust your instincts, you can't really do it wrong.

Because the body believes that all things invisible are "not real", it's important to give it a tangible way of experiencing your non-physical support. The easiest way to open your body to the existence of your Soul or Support Being is to focus on it's presence in the air around you. **Knowing** that it's in the air around you (because it is) and then breathing it into your body creates a very real, physical experience for your body. Now your body will allow the integration or inflow of information and energy that your invisible Support Being can provide.

The next step is to focus on the emotion or issue that you want to eliminate or change. ***Allowing your Support Being to experience it with you*** is the act that creates the transformation.

At this point, it's important to understand that your body does not use thoughts to communicate, it uses *feelings*. When you are working to change what the body is holding, it will be done on the feeling level. If you want to change your response to another person's negative behavior, for instance, then you must focus on how their behavior makes you feel. Focusing on what you think about the issue will not change your body's reaction. Focusing on how you *feel* about the issue allows your Support Being to focus on it as well. When this happens, you will create the higher perspective co-existing with the lower perspective of the body. When you do this, you are creating the reality of the lower emotions being replaced by the higher perspective. In other words, you are creating a healing.

As you continue to hold your attention on the feelings concerning the issue and as you continue to allow your Higher Support to "feel it with you", you will notice a reduction of the emotion. At this point you will either arrive at a new realization concerning the issue, creating a feeling of completion, or you will find yourself experiencing another stronger emotion.

Experiencing another emotion means that you have moved to a deeper level of the issue. Reconfirm that your Support Being is still in your body with you and continue to hold your attention on the new feeling. ***With your Support Being,*** continue focusing on each new emotion as it arises until there are no more and you experience a sense of peace. Take a few moments continuing to be aware of your Higher Support's presence in your body, allowing it to finish its work. An unconscious intake and exhale of air will usually alert you to the fact that the Process is complete.

You can use this Process as a form of meditation, taking 15 or 20 minutes to quietly work with the issues or emotions that you want to heal. You can also use it as the issues surface. In any moment that you realize that you are experiencing a negative response to something, you can remember your Support Being or Soul in the air around you and breathe it into everything that you are feeling. In this way you can neutralize your negative response and replace it with a higher perspective of whatever is occurring. In this way, you can replace your body's primate reactions with your Soul's perspective. In this way, you can achieve a higher level of consciousness in day-to-day situations.

Using The Basic Process this way will also teach your body a new way of responding to life's negativity. More importantly, it gives it a new relationship to negativity; a sense of being equal to it. When your body no longer sees negativity as a potential threat, it can "rise above it". In other words, the use of this Process gives your monkey wings to fly and the freedom to use them.

Summary

BODY PERSPECTIVE	+	SOUL PERSPECTIVE	=	NEW HUMAN PERSPECTIVE
Anger	+	Wisdom	=	Understanding
Fear for Others	+	They are also Soul	=	Compassion & Peace with their creation.
Fear for Self	+	The Power of the All-ness is inherent within	=	Peace
Grief	+	They are also Soul and Soul is forever	=	Peace
Guilt	+	My Nature is Love	=	Forgiveness
Hate	+	My Nature is Love	=	Peace
I Can't	+	The Power of the All-ness is inherent within	=	I will
I'm Not Good Enough	+	The Power of the All-ness is inherent within	=	I am sufficient
Indecision	+	Wisdom	=	Appropriate Choices
Judgement	+	Wisdom	=	Appreciation for the choices of others
Loneliness	+	I am Part of All	=	Peace
Phobias	+	The Power of the All-ness is inherent within	=	Freedom
Regret	+	The Higher Purpose	=	Self Forgiveness
Resentment	+	The Higher Purpose	=	Forgiveness
Self Judgment	+	My Nature is Love	=	Self Love & Self Acceptance

Process Preparation

The are a few things to do before you begin this process that will ensure a more productive and healing experience for you:

➢ Have tissues and a glass of water close at hand.

➢ Give yourself at least 20 minutes with absolutely nothing else to do but *your* healing.

➢ Choose which Support Being you want to support you. (This can be Christ, an Angel or your Higher Soul Self for instance.) It is important to choose a Being that your body is comfortable and most open to. Often an individual will want to work with God, but in truth, their body doesn't trust something that big. Take some time focusing on those Beings that you are interested in or know about and notice which causes your body to be most relaxed. Say the name of the Being and imagine breathing that Being into your body. An indication that your body is not comfortable with your choice is a sense of tension across the shoulders or chest. A "yes" to your choice will usually result in the taking of a deep breath and finding that you are beginning to relax.

➢ Choose the issue that you most want to heal at that moment in your life. Find the most intense emotion associated with the issue and use it as your point of focus in the process. Remember, the more clearly you experience the *feeling*, the more complete your healing will be.

Process Procedure

Weiss Transformation Process One – The Basic Process

➤ Take a few minutes to relax your body.

➤ Focus on your Support Being as it exists in the air around you.

➤ Breathe your Support Being into your body. Confirm your willingness to allow it to co-create only healing and higher Truth with you.

➤ Remember the negative emotion or issue that you wish to heal.

➤ Focus on your feelings regarding the emotion or issue, going as completely as you can into the experience.

➤ Allow your Support Being to experience the feelings with you.

➤ Continue to share any additional emotions or feelings that may surface, until there is a sense of release and peace.

➤ Ask your Support Being if there is anything else you should know about the subject and allow yourself to be open to it's inspiration. (Very often this information will be in the form of feelings or a sense of something rather than in formed thoughts.)

➤ When you feel complete with this communication, thank your Support Being for its support.

➤ Notice how differently you feel about the issue now.

➤ Thank your body for allowing you this experience and acknowledge yourself for your efforts on your own behalf.

Doing Pages

Practice List for Weiss Transformation Process One – the Basic Process

Using a separate sheet of paper and taking your time, record as honestly as you can your answers to the questions below. (There are no right or wrong answers. This is simply an opportunity for you to know more about you.)

1. List 3 things that you don't like about *yourself* and would change if you could.

2. List 3 things that you don't like about *your life* and would change if you could.

3. List 3 things that you don't like about *the world* and would change if you could.

4. What is the one thing that other people do that always upsets you?

5. What is the one thing that you do that always upsets you?

6. What is the worst thing you've ever done to someone else?

7. What is the worst thing someone else has done to you?

8. What is the most embarrassing thing that's ever happened to you?

Home Work Page

Practicing The Basic Process

This Home Work Page is designed to create the opportunity for you to see how The Basic Process works in your life. It's also to support you in becoming more consciously aware of exactly how your Support Being's perspective might affect your perspectives. Set some time aside each day to practice using The Basic Process on the following:

➤ Your answer to Question #7 on your Practice List

➤ Your third answer to Question #3 on your Practice List

➤ Your answer to Question #8 on your Practice List

➤ Your answer to Question #6 on your Practice List

➤ Your first answer to Question #3 on your Practice List

➤ Remember, when doing the Process, it's important to focus on how you feel, not what you think, about each of these issues. At the end of each session, record your experience in your Basic Process Practice Log

The following is an example of a possible Log entry:

MY PRACTICE LOG FOR THE BASIC PROCESS

Nov. 03 Thursday

The Higher Support Being working with me was: my Angel

The Process lasted: about 15 minutes

My Issue: The most embarrassing thing that's ever happened to me was once when I was 7 years old some older boys pulled my pants down at school.

The emotions that I felt were:

anger: because they shouldn't have done that

ashamed: because everyone could see "that part of my body". and because they laughed at me .

afraid: that they might do it again.

angry: at myself because I didn't think that I could stop them from doing it again.

fear: that if I told my teachers they might laugh at me too or if I told my parents that they might get angry at me for letting it happen.

lonely: because they all laughed, I had no one to talk to about it.

The Process:

I let the Angel feel the anger at the boys and it became resentment.

I let the Angel feel the resentment and I remembered my older brother always doing mean things to me. I kept showing the Angel how I felt about that until I could look at everything my brother did with a sense of calm; as if it just wasn't important anymore.

I let the Angel feel how ashamed I was about that part of me being naked and I remember feeling the same way in other situations throughout my life. I stayed focused on the shame until I felt calm about "that part of my body" being exposed. At this point I got "tired" and decided to do the rest of the process on this issue tomorrow.

The Results:

I don't get so angry when I think about what happened but I know that there's more to do around this memory and I look forward to finishing it.

Additional Notes:

I was surprised at how strongly I still felt about this memory after all these years.

I had a very strong feeling that my Angel "enjoyed" it each time that I got to a place of calm.

Even if this is all just my imagination, I realize that I'm able to release negative emotions while "imagining my Angel feeling it with me" so I'd like to see what else I can do with this Process.

CHAPTER FOUR

Creating Wings – Part Two

If the Soul is what connects us to the all-knowing Source then it must also contain wisdom. How wise would I be if I could see with the eyes of my Soul? ...and what would my life be like?

In Chapter Two, we created the image of a huge reservoir of All-Knowing Mind pouring itself down through a very long funnel. We imagined that the All-Knowing Mind was God and that the long funnel was the Soul. In this way we created a picture that helps us to understand how the Soul both connects us to the Source and makes the wisdom of Source available to us. In this chapter, I would like to expand on that image and explore the specific Soul perspectives available to us. We will also take a closer look at the "practical human application" of these perspectives.

Opening to the vastness of our Soul can be a little intimidating for our primate body. That's one of the reasons so many people go "out of body" or "into states of bliss" when this level of Soul alignment is achieved. Remember, one of the genetic bits of information that our body holds to be true is "if it's bigger than me, it could be a threat", and the Soul is definitely perceived as being bigger than our body. When trying to integrate the perspective of the Soul into a specific memory or emotion, it's easier for the body to allow this if we can work with just one part of the Soul. Toward this end, it

61

may be beneficial to perceive the Soul as being a multi-dimensional phenomenon. That is to say a thing of many dimensions; each dimension having a different perspective that the body can use in its healing.

To more completely understand this concept, you can think of the Soul as a Rainbow, each color being a different dimension. In this work, we imagine that there are 99 dimensions of Soul, and the 100th dimension is the All-knowing Source Itself. (100 is an arbitrary number used to give us a sense of the vastness of the Soul.)

Each dimension can be seen as a separate set of frequencies of light, sound and perspective. In the higher frequency dimensions, these three things are experienced as one. In the lower frequency dimensions, they are experienced as separate phenomenon. God, the All-knowing Source, is the highest frequency of light/sound/perspective possible.

The human primate body is designed to provide the Soul with an experience of the 3rd dimension; with realities not available in the higher dimensions. Here the concept of death is possible along with fear, anger, regret, isolation and, perhaps the most interesting concept of all, self-judgment. Love can be seen as something done separately. Joy and peace can be intermittent. Beauty can be experienced as a contrast to something entirely unknown in higher realms; non-beauty or ugliness.

To a Being whose primary sense of its self is of Oneness and being eternal, this 3rd dimensional realm offers wonderful opportunities of expression. I know this isn't how it feels as we go through some of the more negative "opportunities" but that is one of the things that this book is about; learning the Soul's ability to appreciate and be in peace with the negative. Doing this actually diminishes the negative and replaces it with the positive.

In the same way that our 3rd dimensional body is designed

to provide a 3rd dimensional experience, our 4th dimensional body is designed to provide a 4th dimensional experience. Our physical form has five senses for perceiving and data gathering. Our 4th dimensional form has three senses for this same purpose. It can hear the 4th dimensional frequencies of sound. It can see the 4th dimensional frequencies of light. It can see other 4th dimensional forms. It also is capable of "seeing" the energy of thought and emotion.

Although this higher frequency body is beyond the range of our five senses, we do however, frequently include it in our daily living. When meeting someone for the first time, we will decide whether or not we are comfortable with them by judging how they *feel* to us. This ability to "feel" isn't achieved with the sense of touch. It is achieved with the use of one of the 4th dimensional body's senses; it's ability to perceive anger or aggression levels in the other person. In addition to the conscious and unconscious physical cues, our body will use 4th dimensional data to determine how comfortable (or safe) a person is.

Walking into a room and feeling uncomfortable is another example of our physical form responding to 4th dimensional data. A room usually *feels* uncomfortable because of the negative emotional charges that have been left behind there. Concentration camps are another place where the 4th dimensional emotional charges can very easily be "felt".

Some people use their 4th dimensional eyes to see the energy of an illness in a physical form. People who do this are called Medical Intuitives, (although I know many doctors who do this who either aren't aware that they're doing it or they just don't like to talk about it.) Some therapists use "their other eyes" to look into their client's subconscious to gather information in order to support the client in healing a trauma or abuse more quickly or completely.

Obviously, the 3rd dimensional brain has the capacity to make 4th dimensional information usable. There is, in fact, one particular lobe of the brain used for just this function. The information is then sent to a part of the right brain and is perceived as a "visual" or a "knowing". Most often, our use of this information is a totally unconscious event done automatically by the body. As we evolve, however, we are becoming more aware of our ability to consciously use our 4th dimensional senses.

In this work, we will refer to the higher dimensional bodies as either "User Bodies" or "Perspective Bodies" depending on their primary relationship with or influence on our 3rd dimensional form. From this point of view, the 4th dimensional body is seen as a "User Body" in that we use the information that it provides us.

Our 5th dimensional body, however, is very different. These bodies have much less definition and are often experienced as "robed in light". In this realm, we perceive ourselves and our reality without any of the primate perspectives that come with our 3rd dimensional body. In this realm, we do not comprehend the concept of death because we know that ultimately, there is no end to us; only continuing and increased self-knowing. We do not comprehend fear because we are equal and connected to everything. We do not comprehend judgment because everything has a purpose and is therefore necessary. We are not capable of self-judgment because we know that we are The Source expressing Itself. We are not capable of loneliness because we are completely aware of just how connected we are to everything else. Love is not something that you would put a word to in this realm, because it's the only way you can experience. Our 5th dimensional body is a Perspective Body in that it has a perspective that we can use to benefit our 3rd dimensional experience.

The 6th dimensional body is considered to be a User Body. It is the body that we use to explore Time. This body is not anchored in a linear relationship to Time and is therefore free to experience or "travel" to other times both in the past and in the future. Its use is not pertinent to the work that we are doing in this book so additional details regarding its reality are unnecessary here.

Our 7th dimensional perspective, however, is extremely pertinent to the work that we are doing in this book. In this realm, non-judgment and the appreciation for every experience is taken to another level. Here we have the greater understanding of the "why" behind every experience. It is this dimensional aspect of our Soul that can give us the reason for the negative situations and events that occur in our 3rd dimensional lives. Although love is again the primary experience in this dimension, a truly deep sense of peace also permeates this realm.

The forms of the 8th, 9th, 10th and 11th dimensions are used by the 12th dimensional Soul expression as it perceives or influences lower dimensional experience. These Soul Aspects are not pertinent to the work that we are doing in this book so additional details regarding their realities are unnecessary here.

The 12th dimensional perspective of the Soul includes the greater understanding of the purpose of our life in the 3rd dimension. It is that part of us that comprehends the interconnectedness of everything that we experience. Enthusiasm for our plan and joy with the Plan's unfoldment are the primary experiences in this Soul Expression.

Appreciation for those who support us in creating the 3rd dimensional form of the Plan is also a very strong experience here. This appreciation is felt for those who support us in creating the negative as well as the positive. Remember, there is no judgment in these higher realms and this is probably one of the most difficult and most powerful perspectives that this Soul Aspect can share with our 3rd dimensional body.

The Aspects delineated here are the ones used most frequently in our work with the WTP's. The remaining pertinent dimensional Soul Aspects will be discussed in later chapters. This dimensional outline as it is presented in this work is an arbitrary way of looking at the Soul. It is designed to support us in integrating the sometimes overwhelming perspective of the Soul into our human primate body.

Another way of supporting the body in being more receptive to the Soul's perspective and influence is to create an easy way for the body to make the Soul "real". Because our bodies (and our minds) tend to question the validity of most things that are invisible, it becomes necessary to make the Soul more "solid". One way of doing this is to *feel* the Soul in the air around you. Although we intellectually understand that the Soul is probably in and around us, this intellectual understanding isn't enough to make the Soul real for the body.

Sometimes using the imagination can help in creating the necessary relationship between the body and the Soul. Then taking the next step of "breathing the Soul into the body" truly gives the body an experience of the Soul as something working with it. Again, this procedure is intended to create the necessary bridge between your body and your Soul so that *you* can create the kind of change and healing that you desire.

As our bodies are programmed to judge, non-judgmental ways of looking at things can be difficult to understand, much less incorporate as a way of living. How can bad things be acceptable? How can suffering be okay? How can our primate body be accept situations or people that appear to threaten it? And how can we love our enemy and how can we truly forgive things like rape or murder? As our bodies are currently programmed, these ideas can be mentally adopted but the total integration of them seems nearly impossible. Yet the replacement of non-judgment with love is necessary for the survival of our species. As long as we continue to fear, avoid or fight on any level, we cannot achieve anything but temporary and fragile moments of peace on this Earth.

If we are to survive and evolve, another perspective and another way of doing things must be integrated into the body.

The Animating Beingness that animates these human primate bodies is the thing that holds our answers. It is to this Beingness that we must turn, not just in prayer or in meditation, but for a new partnership. A partnership that allows the higher perspectives to become not only how we are, but who we are.

The model of Soul delineation described in this book and the ideas behind the Weiss Transformation Processes were created as a way to achieve this partnership. Everything here is designed to support you in creating your new Human Body and a new *truly* peaceful and joyful way of being. The following Doing and Home Work Pages will provide you the opportunity to practice using your various higher dimensional Soul Aspects so that you can discover for yourself the practical application of their perspectives in *your* life.

Summary: Soul Delineation

3rd Dimensional Reality

Form:

➤ is experienced as solid within the 3rd dimension.

➤ experiences itself as separate from other forms.

➤ is capable of being influenced by higher dimensional perspectives .

➤ is capable of integrating higher dimensional information.

Perspective:

➤ self is separate from the Source resulting in the experience of Self Judgment.

➤ the death of the body is considered the end of Self resulting in a primary reality of Fear.

➤ reality is predominately based on the struggle for survival.

➤ is influenced by the concept of Duality resulting in the experience of Judgment of others.

➤ is capable of intermittent positive emotions: Love and Compassion.

Purpose:

➤ provides Soul with the opportunity to experience itself in a 3rd dimensional reality.

➤ provides Higher Soul Aspects with the opportunity to influence 3rd dimensional reality.

4th *Dimensional Reality*

Form:

➢ is experienced as solid within the 4th dimension.

➢ experiences itself as separate from other forms.

➢ supports the 3rd dimensional conscious and unconscious minds with 4th dimensional information.

➢ can provide the 3rd dimensional mind with a form for Out-Of-Body experiences.

➢ is capable of integrating higher dimensional information

➢ can provide an interim experience for the 3rd dimensional conscious mind after the death of it's body. This interim experience will continue until the next 3rd dimensional incarnation or until the 3rd dimensional conscious mind is sufficiently evolved and the Soul no longer desires lower dimensional experiences.

Perspective:

➢ when providing the 3rd dimensional conscious mind with an interim experience, usually reflects the perspective of the 3rd dimensional mind, but can be influenced by higher dimensional perspectives.

Purpose:

➢ provides Soul with the opportunity to experience itself in a 4th dimensional reality.

➢ provides Higher Soul Aspects with the opportunity to influence 3rd and 4th dimensional reality.

5th Dimensional Reality

Form:

➤ is experienced as formed light within the 5th dimension.

➤ experiences itself as having a connection with but remaining separate from other forms.

➤ is capable of comprehending and using higher dimensional perspectives .

➤ is capable of integrating higher dimensional information.

Perspective:

➤ self is connected to the Source resulting in the experience of Love.

➤ reality is predominately based on the understanding that there is a purpose for everything resulting in the experience of Non-judgment .

➤ includes an appreciation of the reality of Duality

Purpose:

➤ provides Soul with the opportunity to experience itself in a 5th dimensional reality.

➤ provides Higher Soul Aspects with the opportunity to influence 3rd ,4th and 5th dimensional realities.

7th Dimensional Reality

Form:

➢ is experienced as formed light within the 7th dimension.

➢ experiences it's self as having a connection with but remaining separate from other forms.

➢ is capable of comprehending and using higher dimensional perspectives .

➢ is capable of integrating higher dimensional information.

Perspective:

➢ self is connected to the Source resulting in the experience of Love.

➢ reality is predominately based on knowing the purpose for everything resulting in the experience of Appreciation and Peace.

Purpose:

➢ provides Soul with the opportunity to experience itself in a 7th dimensional reality.

➢ provides Higher Soul Aspects with the opportunity to influence 7th and lower dimensional realities.

12th Dimensional Reality

Form:

➢ is experienced as formed light within the 12th dimension.

➢ experiences itself as individual with a higher connection to other forms.

➢ is capable of comprehending and using higher dimensional perspectives .

➢ is capable of integrating higher dimensional information.

Perspective:

➢ self is a flow of the Consciousness of Source resulting in the experience of Oneness-with-All.

➢ reality is predominately based on knowing the **collective** intention for lower dimensional experiences resulting in the experience of Enthusiasm.

➢ reality is also based on the gratitude for all individuals and situations contributing to the lower dimensional experiences resulting in the experience of Joy .

Purpose:

➢ provides Soul with the opportunity to experience itself in a 12th dimensional reality.

➢ provides Higher Soul Aspects with the opportunity to influence 12th and lower dimensional realities.

Doing Pages

Getting To Know Your Dimensional Soul Aspects

Use the following Process to take some time to formally introduce your body to your 5th, 7th and 12th dimensional Soul Aspects. Focus on just one of your Soul Aspects each time you do the process. 20 minutes is a comfortable amount of time to spend with each process.

➤ Take a few minutes to relax your body.

➤ Focus on the specific dimensional Soul Aspect (5th 7th or 12th) as it exists in the air around you. (Ultimately, all your Soul Aspects are "in the air around you". It's not necessary, however, to worry about focusing on the right one. Your Soul knows exactly what your intention is here, so will respond with the dimensional aspect appropriate for your use. Remember too, that "you" are the only thing that your Soul is doing and it is very supportive and enthusiastic about what you are doing.)

➤ As you continue to experience the Soul Aspect in the air around you, begin to breathe it into your body. Continue breathing it in and show it your willingness to allow it to co-create a relationship of Truth and healing with your body.

➤ Take a few minutes to notice what this Soul Aspect feels like in your body. (For some, the experience is very strong. For others, the experience is very subtle. It may also vary each time you do this Process.)

➤ Share with this Soul Aspect anything that you would like it to know.

➤ Ask your Soul Aspect if there is anything that it would like you to know and allow yourself to be open to its inspiration. (Very often this information will be in the form of feelings or a sense of something, rather than in formed thoughts.)

➢ When you feel complete with this communication, thank your Soul Aspect for its support.

➢ Take another few minutes to notice what this particular Soul Aspect feels like in your body.

➢ Thank your body for allowing you this experience and acknowledge yourself for your efforts on your own behalf.

➢ Take a deep breath to end the Process.

Home Work Page

Practicing The Basic Process

Using Specific Soul Aspects

This Home Work Page is designed to create an opportunity for you to experience the different types of support provided by each of your higher dimensional Soul Aspects. In these practice sessions, you will be using a variation to the Basic Process. Before you begin each session, choose one of the following answers from your Chapter 3 Practice List (on page 56) to focus on in your Process:

1. Your second answer to Question #3.

2. Your third answer to Question #2.

3. Your first answer to Question #1.

4. Your second answer to Question #1.

5. Your answer to Question #4

Then proceed with your Process as follows:

1. Begin the Basic Process as usual using your 5th dimensional Soul Aspect as your Support Being and continue the Process until you have a sense of completion.

2. Begin the Process again using your 7th dimensional Soul Aspect as your Support Being. Focus on the same issue and continue the Process until you have a sense of completion.

3. Begin the Process again using your 12th dimensional Soul Aspect as your Support Being. Focus on the same issue and continue the Process until you have a sense of completion.

4. Spend a few minutes noticing the difference in the support

and perspective of each of the Soul Aspects.

5. Complete your Basic Process session in the usual way.

At the end of each session, record your experience in your Basic Process Practice Log.

CHAPTER FIVE

On the Wings of Time

Have you ever heard yourself say "I wish I knew then what I know now?" Well you can!

We are accustomed to thinking of Time as a linear series of events stretching out away from us in two different directions. The Past, what we have already experienced, is somehow "behind" us. The Future, what we have yet to experience, is "ahead" of us. The Past is thought to be accessible to us because it continues to exist in the form of memories and emotions that are stored in the body and the brain. The Future, on the other hand, is thought to be unknown and inaccessible to us because it hasn't yet become "data in our brain". If this were true, however, then accurately predicting future events would be impossible. The fact that accurate future predicting does frequently occur, means that some other phenomenon is available to us. Psychics who are able to accurately see past events for others is another indication of that same "other phenomenon".

Is it possible to change our Past? Yes, of course. The Basic Process, for instance, allows us to do this. Each time that we eliminate a negative emotional memory stored in the body, we are in effect changing our experience of the Past. Each time that we change a learned negative belief system, we are changing the effect that our Past has on us. If the Past is seen as an accumulation of stored electro-chemical information, then, yes, it is possible to change our Past by changing that information.

Changing the Future, however, is a completely different subject because it does not exist as stored information. Is it possible to access "what the Future knows" and use it for healing and transformation today? Is it possible to reach through or across Time in order to access and use future information?

Imagine that you are one of 12 people sitting around a very large dinner table and that each person has a serving dish of one kind of food in front of them. Each takes a portion of the food and passes the dish on to the person next to them. Imagine that you notice a bowl of sweet potatoes across the table from you. You really like sweet potatoes, but only with melted butter. You realize that if you wait for the sweet potatoes to make their way around to you, they will be too cold for the butter to melt on them. This could be a terrible event and is unacceptable to you. You reach across the table, take one of the sweet potatoes out of its bowl and place it on your plate where it happily melts the butter for you. Now all is right with the world and you are in peace again.

As multi-dimensional Beings, we are not limited to the body's abilities or its way of perceiving. As multi-dimensional Beings we have the ability to tap into that part of ourselves that is capable of interacting with the Future. We can reach across, access and use information that exists in other times, in other dimensions and in other parts of our incredibly ancient, eternal, all-knowing Self.

We know from our work with The Basic Process that our bodies are receptive to what the Soul knows. The use of a Future Self as a point of reference is just one more example of this. The second of the WTP's, the Time Process is not meant to be used as a way of discerning or predicting future events. It is to be used when a future perspective would be helpful in resolving problems or issues that currently exist for you. For instance, in a situation that seems overwhelming, being given a sense of the problem as already being resolved can create some peace for you. Asking your Future Self how you resolved the problem or asking if there was anything it would have done differently, is also extremely helpful.

I understand that this use of Time is a bit of a challenge to our linear way of thinking, but it is the basis for the Time work that we will be doing in this book. Increasing the positive in our Present by changing the negative in our Past is something we can do now. It is also something that we can do "now" with our Future. Another potentially challenging thought is; if you, the Present Self, is benefited by working with a Past Self, wouldn't your Future Self be benefited by working with you, it's Past Self?

The Time Process has two applications. The first application is the Future Self working with you in the Present and is done the same way as The Basic Process with one exception. In addition to breathing your 5th dimensional Soul Aspect into your body, you will also allow a Future Self to work with you. This will be a "You" that exists either one or three years from now. (Working with a Self existing more than three years in the future sometimes presents the body with information that isn't as easily understood or accepted.) Together, you and your Future Self will look at a specific problem that is currently occurring in your life to support you in creating a new relationship with the problem.

The second application of The Time Process is done a bit differently. Although you would again breathe the 5th dimensional Soul Aspect into your body and allow your Future Self to work with you, this time, however, the two of you would focus on a time in your childhood that was either traumatic or particularly upsetting. This application is especially effective in healing childhood traumas and in changing negative self-worth believe systems developed during your childhood. (The complete steps to both applications are outlined in the Summary of this chapter.)

Often, in workshops I am asked if our Future or Past selves consciously know that we are communicating with them. The answer for the Past Self is usually "no" because in this Process, the work is actually done in their dream state. The child may remember dreaming something very nice, but for the most part, isn't consciously aware of the support that you are "sending back" to him or her.

The Future Self, however, can be very aware of your interaction. I have had reports of individuals suddenly realizing, while in meditation or day dreaming, that a Past Self was asking them a question. They later remembered that it was the same question that they'd asked a Future Self a few years ago while doing The Time Process. For the most part, they found themselves giving the same answers that they had received. Occasionally, however, they found themselves either giving a more complete answer or they found themselves working harder to help the Past Self feel more loved, empowered or peaceful. We've been teaching the Time Process since 1994 and it's very interesting that we're now beginning to get reports from the "then" Future Selves.

There are those who will doubt that working with a Future Self is possible. Working with or changing something that hasn't happened yet is just too difficult to accept. For these people it might help to look at the subject in another way. Whether we are actually working with an "us" that exists in the future or whether we are working with our imagination, we are still accessing Soul information that can support us in our healing and transformation. Keep in mind that both your intention to heal and your Soul's abilities are very powerful.

Is your Soul feeding perspectives and information to you through your imagination or through a Future Self? Time will tell.

Summary

Process Procedure

Weiss Transformation Process Two – The Time Process

First Application

➢ Take a few minutes to relax your body.

➢ Decide which issue or problem you would like to resolve in this session. (Be specific)

➢ Decide which Future Self you would like to have work with you. It's most effective to work with a Self that exists either one or three years from now. (Trust your intuition on this, you can't really do it wrong.)

➢ Focus on your 5th dimensional Soul Aspect as it exists in the air around you.

➢ Breathe this Soul Aspect into your body, confirming your desire to allow it to co-create healing and higher Truth with you.

➢ Allow yourself to experience your Future Self standing beside you. Be aware of its willingness to work with you. Take a moment to feel comfortable with the presence of this Self. (The experience of the Future Self may be very strong or very subtle. It may also vary each time you do this Process)

➢ Focus on the issue or problem, allowing the Future Self to "see" it with you.

➢ Remember your 5th dimensional Soul Aspect's support and then begin to open to your Future Self's communication. (Very often this information will be in the form of feelings or a sense of something rather than in formed thoughts. You may suddenly have an "idea" of specific things to do about the problem or you may find yourself realizing that it's not as big an issue as you thought.) Take your time with this part of the Process, as you continue allowing the 5th dimensional Aspect to work with your body.

➤ When you feel complete with the Process, ask your Future Self if there's anything else that it would like to tell you and wait a few minutes, giving it the opportunity to do so.

➤ Take another moment and allow yourself the experience of how this Future "you" feels in *it's* body. Is it peaceful? How secure or loved does it feel? Is it content with it's existence? Is it happy with it's degree of healing? What else, if anything would this Future Self change if it could?

➤ When you feel complete with this experience, thank your Future Self for its support and release it back to it's own time.

➤ Take a moment to notice how differently you feel about the problem or issue.

➤ Thank your Soul Aspect for its support and thank your body for allowing this experience. Acknowledge yourself for your efforts on your own behalf.

Second Application

➤ Take a few minutes to relax your body.

➤ Decide which negative childhood experience or trauma you would like to work with in this session. (Be specific.)

➤ Decide which Future Self you would like to have work with you. It's most effective to work with a Self that exists either one or three years from now. (Trust your intuition on this, you can't really do it wrong.)

➢ Focus on your 5th dimensional Soul Aspect as it exists in the air around you.

➢ Breathe this Soul Aspect into your body, confirming your desire to allow it to co-create healing and higher Truth with you.

➢ Allow yourself to experience your Future Self standing beside you. Be aware of its willingness to work with you. Take a moment to feel comfortable with the presence of this Self. (The experience of the Future Self may be very strong or very subtle. It may also vary each time you do this Process)

➢ Focus on the childhood negativity as it occurred, allowing the Future Self to "see" it with you. Quietly observe your younger Past Self as it goes through the experience.

➢ Shift your focus and find the child asleep on the night immediately after the event, using your imagination if you need to. Quietly observe the sleeping child, noticing any tension in the body. You are going to communicate with this Past Self through the dream state. In this way, the child's body will be open to the support that you and your Future Self will offer.

➢ Be aware that your Future Self is beginning to communicate the following information to the child: (You may contribute to this communication as well.)

➢ how loved and safe the child is.

➢ how big and strong he or she will become.

➢ how he or she will indeed survive the negative experiences.

➢ how beautiful and perfect the child is.

➢ that he or she is not alone.

➢ At this point, look around the child's room. There will always be the presence of a Guardian Being who is loving and supportive. (The Guardian Being might be an Angel, Christ, or Soul Aspect for instance.) Hold your attention on the Guardian Being. This will help the little sleeping Past Self to become aware of it as well. In this way, it will be easier for the child to handle any additional negativity occurring in his or her life.

➤ Release the child to the love and care of the Guardian Being, returning your awareness to "now" and the Future Self standing beside you.

➤ Remember your 5th dimensional Soul Aspect's support and then begin to open to anything that your Future Self may know about the negative experience or trauma you experienced in your childhood. Take your time with this part of the Process, as you continue allowing the 5th dimensional Aspect to work with your body.

➤ When you feel complete with the Process, ask your Future Self if there's anything else that it would like to tell you and wait a few minutes, giving it the opportunity to do so.

➤ When you feel complete with this communication, thank your Future Self for its support and release it back to its own time.

➤ Take a moment to notice how differently you feel about the problem or issue.

➤ Thank your Soul Aspect for its support and thank your body for allowing this experience. Acknowledge yourself for your efforts on your own behalf.

Doing Pages

Practice List for the Time Process

Using a separate sheet of paper and taking your time, record as honestly as you can your answers to the questions below.

1. What is the most positive memory you have of your childhood?

2. Did this experience have a direct effect on how you felt about yourself?

3. Does it still affect how you feel about yourself?

4. If your answer is yes, then please note how it still affects you?

5. What is the most negative memory you have of your childhood?

6. Did this experience have a direct effect on how you felt about yourself?

7. Does it still affect how you feel about yourself?

8. If your answer is yes, then please note how it still affects you.

9. At what age were you the happiest and why?

10. At what age were you the most frightened and why?

11. Did anyone ever tell you that you were stupid or would never amount to anything?

12. At what age did you start to believe them?

13. What was the one most positive phrase that you heard most often as a child?

14. Does it still have meaning for you today?

15. What was the one most negative phrase that you heard most often as a child?

16. Does it still have meaning for you today?

17. If you could look back and speak to yourself at the age of five, what would you say?

18. If you could look back and speak to yourself at the age of twelve what would you say?

19. If you could look back and speak to yourself at the age of seventeen what would you say?

20. What is the one thing you wish you could have changed about your childhood?

21. What is the one thing you wish you could have changed about your parents?

22. What is the one thing you wish you could have changed about you?

Home Work Page

This Home Work Page is designed to create an opportunity for you to: 1) see how The Time Process works in your life and 2) become more aware of how your Future Self's perspective might affect your perspectives. In these practice sessions, you will be using the first application of The Time Process. Before you begin each session, choose one of the following answers from your Chapter 3 Practice List (page 56) to focus on in your Process:

a. Your answers to Questions #4 and #5

b. Your answer to Question #8

c. Your answer to Question #18

d. Your answer to Question #19

e. Your answer to Question #20

Then proceed with your first application of the Time Process as outlined in the Summary of this chapter. At the end of each

session, record your experience in your Time Process Practice Log.

The following is an example of a possible Log entry:

MY PRACTICE LOG FOR THE TIME PROCESS

Dec. 03 Thursday

The Future Self working with me was: my 3-year-from-now Self.

The Process lasted: about 20 minutes

My Childhood Focus: Most frightened at 5 years old watching a neighbor's house burn down one night. I remember everyone seemed to be screaming, and the loud noises of the fire trucks hurting my ears.

The Process:

I couldn't feel my Future Self very clearly beside me this time but the calm that comes over my body when it's around did occur as usual.

We began watching my memory of the fire burning the house next door and I realized that what frightened me the most was the lady who lived there screaming over and over "Why is God letting this happen, why is God letting this happen?" As I was re-experiencing the fear I felt my Future Self focusing on my father who was holding me at the time. I felt my father's strength and his arms holding me tightly. I began to realize that my Future Self wanted me to replace my fear with the feeling of my father's quiet strength. I had a difficult time doing that until I remembered to let my 5th dimensional Soul Aspect help me. Then it became very easy. I continued doing this until I could look at the lady and only feel sadness for her. The next thing I realized was the sirens of the fire trucks no longer hurting my ears.

When I asked my Future Self if there was anything else, I didn't get anything at first. Then I suddenly remembered the face of one of the firemen. I remembered I was thinking "What if the fire jumps onto our house, what if God lets this happen to us." (Although I don't think, at that age, I had any idea of what God was.) It was at exactly that moment that a fireman turned and looked at me. I remember the kindness and intensity of his eyes when he said, 'It's OK, you're safe." Then he looked at my father and smiled before walking away. I cried with this memory. I think that this is the first time since that fire that I've truly felt as though there might be someone or something capable of keeping me safe.

The rest of the Process went as usual; yes, my Future Self feels in peace with life; and not as much self love as could be, but we're working on it; and no, there's not anything it would change except to make sure that we keep doing this kind of work, which seems to please my Future Self very much.

The Results:

I'm pleased with my ability to eliminate all the emotion that I used to have around this memory. As usual, I'm surprised at the unexpected perspectives that emerge from doing these processes. I feel very relaxed, as though something very large has been lifted from my shoulders. I want to talk to my father.

Additional Notes:

Dad remembers the fire and the fireman and he shared that he was thinking the same thing when the fireman turned around and said "You're safe". He says that the fireman's face has come back to him many times over the years when he's felt afraid. I think it might have been an angel. Dad says he doesn't believe in angels, just God. Probably shouldn't try to explain my Future Self to him.

I've also noticed that I don't get angry at loud noises any more, or at people (especially women) who are loud.

THE STORY

Part Three

Teach Them What You Know Young Elder

*W*hen he wasn't eating or sleeping, he was up in the highest branches of Lookout Tree. He enjoyed his ability to use his Far-vision to notice the approach of Four-Leggeds at greater and greater distances. It gave him status among his people and they treated him very well. Young Ones would gather around him to hear his "Open Space" stories and their mothers would often bring him food.

He was enjoying his life until he noticed that the other Lookout Elders were beginning to avoid him. They were acting resentfully and jealously towards him. He was confused by this behavior. Why weren't they pleased that one among them was making life easier in their Home? His Far-vision was a good thing. Why should the others be unhappy about it? He didn't know what to do.

As the resentful behavior of the other Lookout Elders increased, he became more and more unhappy. When he tried to speak to them about it, they made hand movements as if to *smack him and moved away from him. He just didn't know what to do. He knew he couldn't abandon his new ability and skill but he hated being treated so badly by his friends.*

When his friend's hostile treatment became more than he could bear, he decided to look for The Eldest One and ask him for his advice. He hunted and hunted for him and finally found him near The Edge looking out into the Open Space. He stood waiting quietly, afraid to disturb the oldest and most forbidding member of his Home. After a very long time The Eldest One spoke without turning around, "Teach them what you know, Young Elder and they won't resent you".

"Yes, of course, thank you", he excitedly responded. "What a wonderful idea", he yelled immediately running back to tell the other Lookout Elders. He didn't see the Eldest One thoughtfully looking after him.

He was very happy when his friends responded to his suggestion with enthusiasm and excitement. He spent many long hours over the next few months showing them how to do what he did. He learned to be very patient with them for Far-vision wasn't as easy for most of them as it was for him. He also learned to teach the ones who learned quickly how to help him teach the ones who learned more slowly. In this way, he didn't have to work so hard and once again could have enough time for his own eating, sleeping, story telling and "looking without looking".

Soon all the Lookout Elders were using their Far-vision and his Home was indeed becoming a very peaceful place in which to live. He was very pleased that this was so. He was also pleased that his friends were once again happy with him. What pleased him the most, however, was hearing The Eldest One say, "You are using your Far-vision wisely Young Elder". Yes, this pleased him the most.

One day, as he was doing his part to keep his Home safe, he noticed something unusual out in the Open Space. When he looked closely, he realized that what he was seeing were several Young Ones moving through the grass beyond the Edge. This wasn't a good thing and he shouted the news to the Elders below. Many of them ran screaming out into the Open Space after the Young Ones. They were herded back into the safety of the Trees with smacks and blows. Everyone was screaming at them "it's dangerous in The Open Space, no one *goes there". Everyone was upset.*

As he watched the chaos below, he remembered his first conversation with The Eldest One. He remembered being told as he stood at the Edge looking out into the Open Space "to go there is to die". He remembered being told that those who ventured out and returned were called crazy and had upset everyone so much that they had to be killed. He wondered if these Young Ones would now have to die too.

He went down into the confusion on the jungle floor. He looked at the faces of everyone around him and saw their fear. He saw the terror in the Young Ones who had caused this and felt sorry for them. They were trying to explain that they were only curious and thought that it was now safe enough to explore beyond the Edge. They thought that the Far-vision of the Lookout Elders gave them the time to explore out in the Open Space. "Far-vision doesn't make you safe", the Elders screamed at the Young Ones, delivering more smacks and blows. "But we only wanted to see", the Young Ones screamed back trying at the same time to shield themselves from their Elders rage.

*Suddenly someone was pointing at him and screaming, "it's all his fault, with his Far-vision". He couldn't believe his ears. They were screaming at him, "it's all his fault, it's all his fault" and running around **him** in frantic circles. He became very afraid and all the confusion and noise began to make him dizzy. He was about to climb back up to his place above it all when he heard The Eldest One cry out over the din, "Stop this, stop this now". Amazingly, everyone did just that and a strange waiting calm spread out over his people. The Eldest One stood and stared at all of them, looking taller than anyone could ever remember, as some would say later. When everyone's attention was finally only on The Eldest One, he said, "It is not safe to leave your Home". There was a pause and then, "You do not have to leave your Home to see what is beyond The Edge. Far-vision is not dangerous. Let there be peace here in our Home." Then The Eldest One did the most unforgettable thing, he said "Young Elder, please teach all of them what you know."*

Teach them What You Know Young Elder

CHAPTER SIX

Will I Be Flying Solo?

Before we go any deeper into this work, I want to take some time to discuss the ramifications of what you are doing in your body, in your relationships and in your life. Up until this point we've been working to eliminate negative emotions and memories that are stored in the body. We've also begun to replace some of the limiting programming that we accepted in our childhood. This work has primarily been about improving the quality of your life; replacing anger and fear with peace; replacing self-judgment with self acceptance. Continued use of these first two Processes will simply increase this for you.

In addition to feeling better in your body and better about yourself, using the Basic Process to neutralize negative responses *as they occur* will create less stress in all of your relationships. Including a Trusted Support Being or Soul Aspect in every negative situation teaches your body a new way of responding. The more eagerly you include the higher perspective in your day-to-day living, the more enjoyable life becomes for you.

For the most part, this will be considered as a good thing by those who interact with you. One possible exception to this, however, are those individuals who have enjoyed engaging in angry exchanges with you, or those who enjoyed eliciting fear responses from you. These people will not be happy with your changes.

Another possible drawback to creating this much change in yourself is that any relationships based on old self-judgments will have to be altered. If the other person in the relationship is not willing to accept a new self (Soul) empowered you, then they may have to be released from the relationship. This, of course, can sometimes be painful. Fortunately, you will know what to do with the pain. You will allow your Trusted Support Being or Soul Aspect to experience it with you and you will move through the pain quickly. In this way you will be ready to create a new relationship with someone who appreciates you for your new qualities.

If improving the quality of your life is enough change for you, then the first two Processes outlined in this book will support you in doing that. If, however, you are wanting something more, then the first two Processes are just the beginning. The work that follows is about becoming something new on the planet. It's about no longer living within the confines of accepted survival-based behavior. It's about becoming a part of a much larger change that is moving through our species. It's about flying above and beyond the "I'm only human" concepts and realities.

Taking responsibility for creating your own life is just one of the things you will have to consider. Accepting your own power to make choices based on *why* you exist is another sometimes difficult task. With the help of your own higher wisdom and with the power of your Soul's intention, you can and will, live the "I'm not only human" reality.

If you are indeed responding to an inner need to become "more", then there are some things that you might want to consider. Until you've replaced a significant amount of your body's primate programming, it will be afraid of what you are doing. You are attempting a significant change. Remember your body's relationship to the word "change"? You are moving into what seems to be a very large unknown; another frightening word. It will be your body's inclination to resist what you are doing.

Resistance can take many forms. Food or substance

cravings are common ways that your body will get you back to doing something "human". Aches and pains are quite effective as a way of keeping you from going too deeply into a process or meditation. Illness will certainly distract you from any spiritual practices unless you know how to use the illness as a way to create the deeper healing. I'm sure you're already aware of just how creative your body can be when it's in survival mode.

As long as your body believes that you are moving towards something that is an "unknown", it must resist what you are trying to create. This is one of the reasons that The Time Process is so helpful. It gives your body a very real sense that the changes you are attempting are not only survivable, but pleasant. Using the second Process frequently and noting the increased peace and sense of personal power (especially in the 3-year-from-now Future Self) helps lessen your body's need to resist.

One of the most unsettling changes for you and your body will be the change in some of the relationships with important people in your life. If you continue taking your trans-formational work to deeper levels and changing your body's programming, you will become more and more "unusual". People in your life who are also working to evolve their bodies will be grateful for your changes and will appreciate your company and your support. They will enjoy discussions about what you are doing. People in your life who are not working to evolve their bodies, however, will begin to think that you are crazy. At the very least, they will begin to avoid you. At the very most, you will be judged, criticized and perhaps even mistreated.

Because we are basically social beings who thrive on the company and acceptance of others, being shunned or criticized can be painful and even frightening. Deep in our DNA is the information that says that we need other humans in order to survive. We do not do well, for the most part, without interaction with others of a like kind. It's not in our human nature to isolate ourselves, although there are those who attempt this as a way of coping with non-acceptance and judgment.

It won't always by easy to distance yourself from those individuals who can't understand or handle "what you're doing to yourself". Even those who do understand may find themselves relating to you differently because your change is activating the fear of change in their body. Especially if they themselves are about to begin major transformational work of their own. You may find that normally very supportive and loving people in your life become confrontational, verbally abusive or distant. There will be times when you think that everyone has either turned on you or abandoned you. You will feel alone. You will feel frustrated because all the healing is supposed to make things better not worse. You *will* feel as though you wish you could just go back to how it was. These feelings may last a few minutes or a few days (depending on how quickly you begin to allow your Soul or Trusted Support Being to work with you to recreate reality in your body). It's usually at this point that a nice long conversation with a Future Self proves beneficial. This will help to make these days of change easier on you.

It is also possible to make your days of change easier for the people around you. There is another way of using the Basic Process that can support them in being more in peace (or at least in less fear) with what you are doing. If you remember, the reason that the Processes work is because of the dynamics of Truth and non-truth co-existing in the same place. As your Soul or Support Being is allowed to co-exist with you in your body, you are actually creating two separate realities in your body; one based on the body's "I'm only Human" and one based on the Soul's "I Am *everything* that I Am". Because the second reality happens to actually be your Truth, it has the power to replace the other reality.   The result, is of course, a reduction in negative responses and an increase in understanding and peace.

You can create the possibility of the same dynamic working in the body of another by doing the same thing that your Soul or Support Being does for you. You have the ability to shift your focus from the negativity that another is sharing with you, to an awareness of their "I Am *everything* that I Am". There are a couple of ways that you can do this. One way is to imagine their Soul or Higher Power stepping into their body and experiencing the negativity with them. Another way is to simply *know* that they are a powerful multi-dimensional Soul in a human disguise. Not only will this minimize your body's negative response to the situation, but your shifted focus will support the Soul of the other in creating the second reality in their body. Then, if a reduction in negativity is appropriate, the other person and their Soul will create it, usually unconsciously.

One of the reasons that we can do this with/for another person is the fact that our bodies have the ability to communicate unconsciously with each other. When you are focused on something that is Truth for another, your body is also focused on that Truth. When your body is focused on that Truth, their body will unconsciously become aware of it as well. (Remember the 4th dimensional communication that we discussed in Chapter 4?) If altering the individual's negativity is something the Soul deems appropriate (if the negativity serves no purpose and is simply a body response), then the Soul will then begin recreating the reality within the individual. This will usually result in a lessening of the negativity. It may also result in a sudden understanding or acceptance of what you are doing.

If you understand that you are holding the focus of Truth for another person to provide them with the option of healing and not because you have a need to reduce their negative response, then you are interacting in the spirit of support rather than in the reality of judgment. In time, experiencing others as an expression of Soul will be your normal way of seeing. This will create the option of healing for others as an automatic response to your being around them.

One of the things that most individuals find themselves doing when they discover their ability to create positive change in the world around them is to think that they *must* create positive change in the world around them. Actually, the world is doing exactly as it should be doing; providing a wealth of experience, both positive and negative, for it's inhabitants. For those who have a Soul intention to create positive change for themselves, our change becomes a support. For those who have a Soul intention to experience the negative (for whatever Soul reason), our change can become a nuisance.

It's really not our job to heal, fix or save. Our only responsibility is to be living the Truth within ourselves, which will eventually include seeing everything for the light and higher expression that it is. Doing this will create the potential for healing or change for those for whom it's appropriate.

Our own transformation work will, of course, touch and effect others. As social creatures, we will share what we are learning and what we are doing. Some of us will find ourselves including this sharing in our work. This may look like teaching or working in some fashion as a facilitator for the healing in others. When this is done in the spirit of non-judgment, then we are co-creating change in the world around us. When this is done in the spirit of judgment or "needing to fix or save", then we find ourselves contributing to the negativity in the world around us.

One of the things that I hear most frequently from my own teachers is "It's not what you do, it's the energy in which you do it that's important." This statement serves as a constant reminder for me to be in peace with other people's choices. It also helps me to be in peace with what I do as a facilitator and teacher. I'm always aware of how difficult this work can be for the ones that I work with. It's not always easy to take them through a Process that I know will be painful. When I focus on who and what they are in essence, then I see their strength and ability to move to the freedom on the other side of the pain. This helps my body to find the courage to do some of the more intense levels of this work with other people. This also helps my body to create a more compassionate and loving environment in which other people may do the more intense work.

Another important application of this for me is in situations when I'm aware of the resistance in the ones that I'm working with. Sometimes the resistance can take the form of anger or a "you can't make me" attitude. In those moments, I look inside for their Soul's intention to use what I'm offering. When I can see what brought them to me in the first place, then they also become aware of it. It's then that their energy shifts and they begin to create healing for themselves.

The most effective and powerful thing that we can do for ourselves and for our world is to create our own transformation; from living as a judgmental being to living as one who is capable of seeing from the Soul's perspective. When we do this, we become examples; we become beacons; we become proof that living as a Soul is something that can be done by a human. We become proof that this level of personal transformation is survivable. And...in the language of the human primate body that we live in, that's a very good thing.

Summary

On The Subject Of Change

Any reduction in the amount of Fear inside of you results in exactly the same amount of Fear being reduced in the world.

Any increase in the amount of Love inside of you results in exactly the same amount of Love being increased in the world.

One way or another you have an effect on your world.

Never underestimate the power of seeing (and appreciating) the Higher Nature of another.

Your way isn't necessarily their way.

They don't need you to fix or save them. They only need you to love them without judgment.

Doing Pages

Practice List for The Basic Process

Using a separate sheet of paper and taking your time, record as honestly as you can your answers to the questions below. You will be using some of your answers to these questions for your Home Work.

1. How long have you been actively working to change "how you are"?

2. How much of what you know about the Soul's perspective do you think you actually live?

3. How often do you ask "why" something is happening?

4. What were the circumstances the last time you asked this question?

5. How often do you feel as though this planet isn't really your home?

6. Have you ever felt as though you wanted to "end it all"?

7. If yes, when was the last time you felt this way and what were the circumstances?

8. How often do you find yourself not discussing your beliefs because you're afraid of what someone else might think?

9. Do you consider yourself to be psychic?

10. If yes, how often do you share this fact with others?

11. If you are psychic (or if you were psychic), who could you talk to about it? List the names of at least five people and why.

12. If you are psychic (or if you were psychic), who could you not talk to about it? List the names of at least five people and why.

13. What is your greatest hope for yourself in this lifetime?

14. What is your greatest fear?

15. When you look at what's happening on the planet, does it please you?

16. Why?

17. When you look at what's happening on the planet, does it distress you?

18. Why?

19. Why is actively working to change "how you are" important to you?

Practice List for the Time Process

Using a separate sheet of paper and taking your time, record as honestly as you can your answers to the questions below. You will be using some of your answers to these questions for your Home Work.

1. Do you believe that it's possible to complete all the healing you need in the next three years?

2. Do you believe that you can truly make a difference on this planet?

3. Why do you believe this?

4. How often in a day do you experience the feeling of Love?

5. How often in a day do you experience the feeling of anger?

6. How often in a day do you experience the feeling of fear?

7. How often in a day do you wish you knew more?

8. Do you believe that the world will be significantly changed in the next three years?

9. Do you believe that you might see a shift in the consciousness of our species in your lifetime?

10. Are you afraid that if you change too much, that you might end up alone?

11. If money weren't a concern, what specifically would you do with your time?

12. If you were in the perfect relationship, what would it look like?

13. What do you think total self-acceptance would look like?

14. What do you think total self-acceptance would feel like?

15. What does unconditional love mean to you?

16. Have you ever given it to another?

17. If yes, to whom and when?

18. If no, why do you think this is?

19. Have you ever received unconditional love from another?

20. If yes, from whom and when?

21. If no, why do you think this is?

22. Would you say that you are in peace with your life?

23. Why?

24. Would you say that you are grateful for this lifetime?

25. Why?

26. What do you think is the one greatest negative this planet has to offer?

27. What do you think is the one greatest positive this planet has to offer?

Home Work Page

Using The Basic Process

This Home Work Page is designed to create an opportunity for you to discover and apply more of your Soul's perspective your life. In these practice sessions, it is suggested that you allow both your 5th and 7th dimensional Soul Aspects to work with you. Before you begin each session, choose one of the following answers from Basic Process Practice List on page 105 to focus on in your Process:

a. Your answer to Question #4

b. Your answer to Question #14

c. Your answers to Questions #17 and #18

d. Your answers to Questions #6 and #7

e. Your answer to Question #2

Then proceed with your Basic Process. At the end of each session, record your experience in your Basic Process Practice Log.

Using The Time Process

This Home Work Page is designed to create an opportunity for you to discover and apply more of your Future Self's perspective to your life. In these practice sessions, it is suggested that you allow your 3 year-from-now-self to work with you. Before you begin each session, choose one of the following answers from your Chapter 6 Time Process Practice List to focus on in your Process:

a. Your answer to Question #14

b. Your answer to Question #10

c. Your answer to Question #15

d. Your answer to Question #24

e. Your answer to Question #19

f. Your answer to Question #27

g. Your answer to Question #8

Then proceed with your Time Process – First Application. At the end of each session, record your experience in your Time Process Practice Log.

CHAPTER SEVEN

If I Change My DNA, What Will I Be?

Is the reason that a monkey cannot fly because its body does not include the appropriate flying apparatus or because it hasn't activated its latent genetic flight manual?

We've discussed the importance of changing "what the body knows" in order to change it's influence on our behavior. In the preceding chapters, we worked with tools for altering limiting childhood and cultural influences. We worked to reduce the accumulation of painful memories and negative emotions stored in our bodies. We've learned how to align with higher sources of insight, wisdom and perspective. Now, in the words of my Teachers, "let's go deeper"; right to our body's building blocks, the DNA.

When the DNA Process was first presented to me, I must say I found myself questioning the sanity of my Teachers. It just didn't make sense to me. The concept also frightened me. I remember saying, "you can't go mucking about with the body's genetic programming. Good Lord, what would we become?" The silence that my Teachers responded with was a hint that I should think about it. So I did and this is what I came up with. Our fear is ultimately based in genetic information. Our fear is not our true nature and it actually stands in our way. Therefore, our fear must be replaced if we are to live our true nature. Therefore, it just might be advantageous to go to the source of the fear. It just might be advantageous to have a DNA Process to work with. When I looked to my Teachers again, I heard "Well done, now are you ready?"

DNA is what tells the body how to construct itself. Human Primate DNA is what tells the body how to continue its existence (to survive). Human Primate DNA is something that has been evolving for a very, very long time. This means that in addition to survival information, evolutionary information is also part of our body. In this work, we will consider another influence that is available to us; the power of Soul intention and intervention.

There are two ways of looking at the necessity and possibility of changing our genetic information. Speaking strictly from a survival perspective, we cannot survive as a species if we don't find a way of modifying our aggressive nature. The planet's population is beginning to grow more quickly than our territorial programming will allow. (The increase in crime rates in big cities is one example of this. The extinction of so many of our planet's other life forms is another example.) We must find another way to be with each other if we are to continue our existence on this planet.

We can either continue on a negative track until we eliminate ourselves, or we can continue on a positive track and create something completely new for ourselves. At this point in time, both intentions appear to be in operation on our planet. The second intention, however, seems to be gaining momentum. The desire for something completely new is growing in our species and it can be seen just about everywhere. Everything is being redefined, including the concepts of God, Spirit, Life, Love, Power and Self. The desire for higher wisdom has become a matter of survival. Who are we? What are we? Why are we? These are the questions that are being asked more and more frequently.

Speaking from a spiritual perspective, it appears as though we're ready to hear the answers. It also appears as though the answers are being found in a place that, as a species, we aren't accustomed to looking for them; inside ourselves. Our "still small voice" is becoming louder and more available. Higher Guidance is becoming Inner Knowing. If you ask your Soul what it wants, it will more than likely tell you that it would like you to be more peaceful. This is not a new answer. Peace and Love have been the Soul's message for some time. However, if you were to ask again, you would find that a new message has been added. The new message is "I would like to be your Partner".

When we begin to create a partnership with our Soul, the first thing we find is that its concepts are difficult to actually live. When we begin to change the necessary paradigms to increase our ability to live the Soul's concepts, we find that it is a slow and difficult process. When we ask the Soul for additional support, it answers "let me in". We answer with "I already have" and it answers again "let me into your body".

The Soul is actively asking for the opportunity to create a conscious partnership in order to evolve the physical form that it animates. In order to do this, we must consciously allow its support and interaction. Although we are willing to do this, its not in our body's nature to recognize or comprehend the Soul. It is therefore necessary for us to create a bridge between the two. The DNA Process takes this "bridging" to another level and allows you and your Soul to include the body in the partnership. This creates empowerment. It also creates the ability to more easily shift the paradigms necessary to allow us to *live* the Soul's perspective. This Process is in one respect a shortcut to creating the kind of life that you've been asking for.

Weiss Transformation Process Three – The DNA Process has two applications. The first application works with the 5th and 7th dimensional Soul Aspects and is designed to neutralize genetic information that holds your body in a fear reality. Remember, it's only your Soul that you are allowing into your DNA. Your Soul would know exactly what information no longer serves you and, when allowed, has the ability and the power to neutralize that information. You can also look at this from the left-brain perspective of the higher frequency Soul reality altering the lower frequency fear reality. Either way, when the Soul is focused into your bones, into your cells, into the DNA, something wonderful happens.

The second application works with the 12th dimensional Soul Aspect and is designed to activate the evolutionary information, what I call the Divine DNA. Evolving is one of the things that life forms do on this planet. Allowing the Soul to access and activate this genetic information supports us in doing it consciously, something that other life forms on this planet don't do. (Although there are rumors that dolphins may know about this.)

We work with the 12th dimensional Soul Aspect in this Application because it is the part of us that completely understands the purpose for this lifetime and this body. It is the Aspect best suited to activate the specific coding which would most support that purpose. This results in less resistance to the shift in consciousness that we are trying to accomplish. It also results in higher dimensional communication being much easier and clearer.

The procedure for The DNA Process is a little different from the other two processes in that once your dimensional Soul Aspects are in place, you will be opening your eyes to do the Process. Again, it's necessary to give your body an experience that not only allows it to be involved, but gives it the sense that something is indeed happening. Toward this end, you will be asked to focus on the palm of your left hand. Using your imagination if you have to, you would then focus into the bones, into the cells and into the DNA. For some, the experience is very visual and the DNA can be seen either as streams of color or as a flow of tiny bits. Next, your Soul would be allowed to begin sending a stream of consciousness or light directly through your hand into the DNA where it would begin it's work to neutralize or activate the appropriate genetic coding depending on which application and Soul Aspect you are using. The following Summary Section of this chapter will have the complete instructions for both applications of The DNA Process.

At this point, I would ask that you take some time to think about the ideas discussed here. Do you believe that it's possible for your Soul, your Higher Power to have such an effect in your body? Is it a matter of your Soul working a miracle for you or can it be that all genetic coding is basically energy in essence and can therefore be changed by applying a higher form of energy, Soul focus? Do you believe that such a thing is possible for you? How important is it in your own spiritual evolution?

What we are evolving into is a new Human. It's not about growing new limbs or changing the way we look. It's about creating a physical form with a subconscious perspective that allows us the freedom to live a life without fear and self-judgment. It's about creating a reality of love and joy and creativity. It's about us finally living what we've always wanted, a world without hate; without suffering, without injustice, without slavery of any kind. It's about experiencing ourselves as a Soul with a body, rather than a body with a Soul. It's in us to do this. It's in us to fly. It's in our bones, it's in our cells, it's in our DNA.

Summary

Process Procedure

Weiss Transformation Process Three – The DNA Process

First Application

This Process may take 5 minutes or it may take 20 minutes. It will be different each time and you will know when the session feels complete.

The most difficult aspect of this Process will be to stay conscious and you may find that your mind will wander. As the Soul is responsible for working with the DNA, you are responsible for keeping your body open to it's work. Your continued attention to the Soul's flow of consciousness or light is the way to do this.

➢ Take a few minutes to relax your body.

➢ Focus on your 5th Dimensional Soul Aspect as it exists in the air around you.

➢ Breathe this Soul Aspect into your body, confirming your desire to allow it to co-create healing and higher Truth with you.

➢ Focus on your 7th Dimensional Soul Aspect as it exists in the air around you.

➢ Breathe this Soul Aspect into your body, confirming your desire to allow it to co-create healing and higher Truth with you.

➢ Open your eyes and begin to focus on the palm of your left hand. Imagine seeing through the skin to the bone; into the bones to the cells; into the cells to the DNA.

➤ Confirm your willingness to allow your Soul to co-crea genetic change for you and begin to allow a stream of it's consciousness or light to flow into the palm of your hand. Visualize the stream flowing through the bones; into the cells; right into the DNA. (Trust whatever visual or sense of this experience that happens for you.)

➤ Continue to stay focused on the flow as it begins to seek out the primate survival coding that no longer serves you.

➤ Continue to stay focused on the flow as it begins to work its way up your arm to the rest of your body. (Some will experience the visual of this happening, others will experience a sensation of warmth.)

➤ Continue to stay focused on the stream of Soul energy as it flows into your hand; into the bones; into the cells; into the DNA as it continues to work its way through your body.

➤ Maintain a conscious awareness of the Soul's flow until it feels complete. At that point, close your eyes and put your hands together.

➤ Take a few moments to breathe quietly while your Soul completes its work with your body.

➤ You may ask your Soul Aspects anything that you would like to know about your Process and be open to their answers.

➤ When you feel complete with this communication, thank your Soul Aspects for their support.

➤ Notice how you feel in your body.

➤ Thank your body for allowing you this experience and acknowledge yourself for your efforts on your own behalf.

Procedure

ransformation Process Three — The DNA Process

Second Application

This Process may take 5 minutes or it may take 20 minutes. It will be different each time and you will know when the session feels complete.

In addition to the 5th and 7th dimensional Soul Aspects, your 12th dimensional Soul Aspect will also be working with you in this Application of the Process. It is this Soul Aspect that fully understands your purpose in this body and is therefore best suited to activate the specific coding which would most support that purpose.

The most difficult aspect of this Process will be to stay conscious and you may find that your mind will wander. As the Soul is responsible for working with the DNA, you are responsible for keeping your body open to its work. Your continued attention to the Soul's flow of consciousness or light is the way to do this.

➤ Take a few minutes to relax your body.

➤ Focus on your 5th Dimensional Soul Aspect as it exists in the air around you.

➤ Breathe this Soul Aspect into your body, confirming your desire to allow it to co-create healing and higher Truth with you.

➤ Focus on your 7th Dimensional Soul Aspect as it exists in the air around you.

➢ Breathe this Soul Aspect into your body, confirming your desire to allow it to co-create healing and higher Truth with you.

➢ Focus on your 12th Dimensional Soul Aspect as it exists in the air around you.

➢ Breathe this Soul Aspect into your body, confirming your desire to allow it to co-create healing and higher Truth with you.

➢ Open your eyes and begin to focus on the palm of your left hand. Imagine seeing through the skin to the bone; into the bones to the cells; into the cells to the DNA.

➢ Confirm your willingness to allow your Soul to co-create genetic change for you and begin to allow a stream of its consciousness or light to flow into the palm of your hand. Visualize the stream flowing through the bones; into the cells; right into the DNA. (Trust whatever visual or sense of this experience that happens for you.)

➢ Continue to stay focused on the flow as it begins to seek out and activate the Divine genetic coding needed to support you in your spiritual work.

➢ Continue to stay focused on the flow as it begins to work its way up your arm to the rest of your body. (Some will experience the visual of this happening, others will experience a sensation of warmth.)

➢ Continue to stay focused on the stream of Soul energy as it flows into your hand; into the bones; into the cells; into the DNA as it continues to work it's way through your body.

➢ Maintain a conscious awareness of the Soul's flow until it feels complete. At that point, close your eyes and put your hands together.

➢ Take a few moments to breathe quietly while your Soul completes its work with your body.

➢ You may ask your Soul Aspects anything that you would like to know about your Process and be open to their answers.

➢ When you feel complete with this communication, thank your Soul Aspects for their support.

➢ Notice how you feel in your body.

➢ Thank your body for allowing you this experience and acknowledge yourself for your efforts on your own behalf.

Doing Pages

Practice List for Talks with Your Soul

Using a separate sheet of paper and taking your time, record as honestly as you can your answers to the questions below. You will be using some of your answers to these questions for your Home Work.

1. What do you think is the primary reason for your life on this planet?

2. List three other reasons for your life on this planet.

3. Do you think that your life is important?

4. Why?

5. What is the one most important thing that you want from your Soul?

6. Why?

7. Is the idea of your Soul co-creating change in your DNA a positive one for you?

8. Why?

9. Do you have any fears about allowing your Soul to do this level of work in your body?

10. Why?

11. Do you doubt your Soul's ability to do this level of work?

12. Why?

13. Do you doubt your ability to allow your Soul to co-create this level of work in your body?

14. Why?

15. What do you think is your Soul's highest desire for you?

16. List any other things that you think your Soul may desire for you.

Home Work Page

Talks With Your Soul

Because working with the DNA can be a frightening thought to the body, it's important that the time be taken to completely understand the motivation for this Process. As it is your Soul that you are opening your body so intimately to, and as it is your Soul who is asking for the opportunity to co-create with you, it is therefore to the Soul that you must go for this support.

Using The Basic Process, ask all three Soul Aspects (5th, 7th and 12th) to participate. You will be using one of the following answers from your Soul Talk List in this chapter as a point of focus for each session.

a. Your answers to Questions #3 and #4

b. Your answer to Question #9

c. Your answers to Questions #11, #12, #13 and #14

d. Your answer to Question #15

e. Your answer to Question #5 and #6

Then proceed with your Basic Process, taking the time to share your answer with the Soul Aspects and to be open to their perspectives on your answers as well. At the end of each session, record your experience in your Basic Process Practice Log.

Note: Asking both Future Selves for their perspective on your use of The DNA Process might prove interesting. If you choose to have this conversation with them, ask each one (in separate sessions) to show you the results of doing this Process and how often they practiced in order to create their results. You might also ask them if there is anything they would have done differently. At the end of each session, record your experience in your Time Process Practice Log.

Practicing The DNA Process

This Home Work Page is designed to create an opportunity for you to see how The DNA Process works in your life. Proceed with your DNA Process – First Application as outlined in the Summary of this chapter. At the end of the session, record your experience in your DNA Process Practice Log.

It is extremely beneficial to give your body a couple of days before practicing the Second Application of The DNA Process. This gives your body an opportunity to integrate and get used to what you and your Soul have created. At the end of your Second Application session, record your experience in your DNA Process Practice Log.

The following is an example of a possible Log entry:

MY PRACTICE LOG for THE DNA PROCESS

Dec. 18, Friday

The Process lasted: about 10 minutes

The Process: First Application

The Results: The session was very different today. Usually I don't feel much but sort of have a sense of sparkles working through my bones. Today I really felt it! It was warm and I was very sure that my Soul was in my bones. Afterwards, I had a sense that my Soul Aspects were pleased because I felt sort of "happy" in my heart. Don't know what other words to use.

Additional Notes: None

MY PRACTICE LOG for THE DNA PROCESS

Dec. 21, Monday

The Process lasted: about 15 minutes

The Process: Second Application

The Results: My 12th dimensional Aspect must be getting stronger or I'm becoming more open to it because I really felt it today in my body. It's like I was "stronger" somehow or more centered in myself. I couldn't keep track of it moving through my body because the energy was so strong that I could only keep my focus on my hand.

Additional Notes: It seems to get easier to stay focused each time that I do the process but I think that it's because I'm experiencing more than when I first started. I guess I don't have to see sparkling lights like some of the others do.

CHAPTER EIGHT

Don't Look Down

One of the first things that we notice about personal transformation work is that it doesn't necessarily make everything better right away. Many of us have been at this for a many years and no matter how effective the tools we use, it seems to be taking a long time for our Shift In Consciousness to actually happen. One of the reasons for this is that we are in what I call, The Realm Of Slow Motion, where for the most part, things do not happen in "the twinkling of an eye". Working day in and day out doesn't always give us the perspective needed to see the changes that we are actually making. If we look back over the last ten, five, even three years, however, we can see that we actually have made some very noticeable changes in ourselves.

The problem isn't that we haven't been creating a new and more positive reality; the problem is that the remaining negativity is being intensified and our attention is being drawn away from the positive. For example, although we get angry less often and the anger doesn't last as long when it does happen, we get very frustrated at the fact that we still get angry in the first place. The frustration at ourselves is becoming more intensified and our overall sense of things is that we haven't made any progress at all.

Another example for some of us is that things around us also seem to be getting unusually intense as well. Either it's people we know developing terminal illnesses, or mechanical and electrical things constantly breaking down or simply that everyone around us seems to be in a constant state of not coping. What in the world is happening and where is our

"Heaven on Earth" that we're supposed to be creating with all the hard work we've been doing on ourselves?

There are many ways of explaining this and I will give you one of those perspectives here. When an individual (or a species) begins the process of transformation, Soul responds with a stream of new and higher frequency energy and perspective. These higher frequency energies and perspectives interact with the collective intention to change. This causes anything and everything that needs to be changed to rise to the surface. The stronger the intention to change, the more powerful the Soul's focus becomes. The more powerful the Soul's focus, the more rapidly things must change. As a result, things can look pretty chaotic for a while.

Although it doesn't look like it, what's happening in our world and in ourselves is actually good news and, in one perspective, a matter of psychological physics. At least half of our planet's population is actively involved in a spiritual shift in consciousness, in one way or another. As the number of individuals beginning the process of changing from Primate to Divine increases on our planet, the demand for new ways in which to regulate ourselves also increases. A power structure based on survival instincts isn't going to answer the new call. A completely new way of responding to and supporting the masses has become necessary. As a result, just about everything on our planet is being questioned. Every governing power is being challenged, whether it's parental, social, religious or economic.

Although our bodies contain the genetic information necessary to accomplish our next physical evolutionary step, they do not, as yet, contain the information necessary to accomplish our next social evolutionary step. Our body's primate nature is the cause of all the individual and global strife in the first place and it's not designed to support us in moving forward into something different. That information must come from our higher nature.

We've been gifted with many sources of Higher Wisdom over the ages. Sages, saints, teachers, avatars, gurus and holy books have all contributed to supporting us in understanding that there is another less negative way to be with ourselves and with each other. Hearing it from somewhere outside ourselves, no matter how holy the source, doesn't seem to be enough, however. We're still struggling with survival behavior. Obviously, **knowing** about higher perspective isn't the same as **being** the higher perspective. Which brings us back to the importance of what this work is about; integrating what the Soul knows into the body in order to change the body's nature. No matter what discipline or set of procedures you use, **integrating** the new perspective into the body's way of being has become necessary.

Because over half of our planet's population is actively involved in a spiritual shift in consciousness, the Heaven on Earth that we've been looking for will, indeed, be created. We can use our Soul's eyes to see that in time, things do begin to sort themselves out; and it is, just a matter of Time. We are, after all, in a plane of existence where Time is a governing factor.

There are, actually, two reasons for taking our time with our individual and planetary transformation. The first reason is due to the fact that the Soul's main purpose for inhabiting a body in this earth plane is for the **experience** of it. Therefore, a full measure of experience is desirable, and rushing the transformational process might mean missing something valuable.

The second reason for taking our time is the human capacity or incapacity for change. The human psyche cannot cope if things around it or in it change too quickly. Because it is, after all, the body that we are transforming, it is very important that we go at the body's pace. It is extremely counterproductive to push the body too quickly and cause it to go insane.

One of the things that will make this less stressful is the use of any process or tool that helps us to achieve peace and non-judgment. Although some think that drugs or alcohol are great ways to achieve this, these things actually bring greater harm to the body. There are many meditative practices available for achieving inner peace, and this is one of the reasons for the creation of the Weiss Transformation Processes.

The process of transition doesn't have to be painful and you don't have to do it alone. It also doesn't have to take forever. Allowing your Soul, your own Higher Power, to go through the experience with you gives you the ability to lessen the pain and to shorten the time that you're in it. Remaining open to your Soul's attention also creates the sense that you are always supported and appreciated; something that we all could use more of.

Another way of supporting your body is by keeping track of the positive changes that you are creating for yourself. The Process Logs in this book, for instance, are designed for that purpose. If you have a clear sense of what you are accomplishing, it will be easier to accept the things you have yet to accomplish.

What you are attempting to create in your life is significant. Changing the basic genetic psychology of the human physical form is an incredible concept. Only something as powerful as God could accomplish this. Fortunately, that awesome and powerful Something Behind Everything is exactly what Souls are made of. Equally as fortunate is the fact that your body has your Soul's full attention. The magic really begins, however, when the Soul has the body's full attention.

To that end, when looking down into your subconscious, take your Soul's focus with you and your subconscious will begin to reflect your Soul's Truth. When looking back into your Past, take your Soul's focus with you and your Past will begin to reflect your Soul's Wisdom. When looking into the eyes of another, look with your Soul's perspective and you will experience your Soul's recognition of another Soul. Make your Higher Power your partner and it will share what it is and what it knows. Breathe it into your body and you will become the Divine Human. Because all Flying Monkeys know you mustn't look down... without the eyes of your Soul.

THE STORY

Part Four

Empower Them, Young Elder

*His days were filled with the excited chatter of Young Ones as they gathered around him. They were eager to learn more about using their Far-vision as he did. He was honored among his people. Never before had any of his kind been in such a position. Never before had any of his kind been asked to teach **all** of the others. This made him the Highest Teaching Elder, one of the most precious of positions among his People.*

He was careful not to use his position unwisely. The Eldest One had cautioned him frequently about that. On more than one occasion, while working with groups of his people up in the high branches of their trees, he would look up to see that he was being observed by their Leader. And on more than one occasion, after a long day of speaking and teaching, he was taken aside and given sagely advise.

He was never sure why this had happened to him but questioning The Eldest One about it never helped. He was always only told, "Because it was time for it to happen". He wondered if he would ever understand that answer. He wasn't sure he really wanted to.

For the most part, his life was very enjoyable. It was nice to be liked and looked up to. And all the attention that he received from the females when they brought him food was certainly an advantage. But there were times when he wasn't so sure about being The Teacher of Far-vision.

There were those among his People who had a very difficult time learning to use their Far-vision and they had given up and blamed him for his inability as a Teaching Elder. There were even a few who didn't want to learn because it wasn't how it should be done. They didn't like the changes that it was creating in their Home. More than once he heard them chattering behind him. And more than once they would become silent when he turned to look at them.

He wasn't afraid of them. He was doing what The Eldest One had asked him to do. It did confuse him, however, and when he had asked The Eldest One about it he was told, "They are afraid". This didn't help his confusion. How could anyone be afraid of being able to see?

The only other thing that had given him trouble was in the early days of his work as a Teaching Elder. As more and more of his People learned to use their Far-vision, the other Lookout Elders became concerned that they would lose their positions of importance. After a conversation with The Eldest One, he decided to make them Teachers too. He taught them his way of working with the others. He taught them to take over for him when the task of "teaching all of them what you know" became too overwhelming. In this way, they maintained their position of uniqueness in the highest branches of Lookout Tree.

With the exception of the silence that a few of his People showed toward him, his life was very happy. He was doing something that benefited his People. He was doing something that pleased The Eldest One. He was doing something that allowed him to use his Far-vision. He was doing something that made him feel important. He was very happy. Until...

One morning the most agonizing scream that he had

ever heard woke him from his dreams. As the scream continued it was joined by other equally upsetting screams. What was going on? He hastily checked to see if a Four-Legged had somehow made it's way into their Home. There was no Four-Legged in their Home. There was something far worse. Death was in their Home. The Eldest One had died.

The confusion and chaos that followed were beyond his comprehension. His People were in an uproar. They beat the ground with their fists and screamed at the trees and at the Sky. They ran in circles around their dead leader's body until they were all exhausted. Then some of the older females began covering the body of The Eldest One with leaves and branches. Others began to throw fruits or berries on top. Everyone felt the need to make a contribution to the Covering Up. He had been their Eldest One for as long as most of them could remember.

Through it all he simply sat leaning up against a tree. His own sense of loss was nearly more than he could bear. How could he continue? What would he do without the guidance of his teacher? What would his People do now?

When it was his turn to throw a contribution on top of

The Covering, he chose some of The Eldest One's favorite berries. In this way he felt that he was somehow giving something back to the one who had given him everything.

The days that followed were filled with grief and confusion. His People began taking their grief out on each other until many had been hurt. There was no one to shout, "Stop this, stop this now" as The Eldest One would have done. His Home wasn't a quiet and happy place any more. Even the highest branches of Lookout Tree didn't afford him solace. Many of the others followed him up there prodding him for answers and direction. Somehow they seemed to think that he could make things better. How he missed having his teacher to tell him what to do.

One evening, when the arguing and fighting below was louder than usual, He decided that something had to be done. Some of the other Elders had come forward trying to take over as a new leader but they were always pushed away by someone bigger or stronger. His People weren't recovering from their loss very well and things were beginning to get very bad. Just that day, six Young Ones were caught going out into the Open

Space to escape the chaos. They wanted to find a new Home. He knew that there wasn't a new Home to go to. There was only this one and they would have to find a way to make things better here.

He began to look out into the Open Space with his Far-vision. He wasn't sure what he was looking for, just something that would give him an idea on how to help his People. Suddenly he knew that someone was on the branch behind him. When he turned to see who was interrupting him, he nearly went unconscious. There was The Eldest One, looking at him the way he always did. He was sure that the grief and fatigue had caused him to lose his mind. The Eldest One smiled and said, "No, you haven't lost your mind. But you might if you don't slow it down. You can see me because you have developed your Far-vision enough to do so. Yes, my body is dead, but I am not. Yes, I am aware of what has been happening in our Home. Yes, there is something that you can do about it. No, you don't have to lead them. You are a Teaching Elder. Teach them new ways to use their Far-vision as you are using yours now. Teach them that there is another way. *Empower them, Young Elder. Teach them what else they need to know. Your Far-vision will guide you. Trust it. Trust yourself. Empower them, Young Elder, so that they may know Peace."*

With a final *"Go to them now"* The Eldest One disappeared from his place on the branch and only the breeze remained to keep him company while he tried to cope with what had just happened. The words *"Go to them now"* repeated in his head and it shook him out of his daze. He began to make his way down the tallest of trees in his Home. He worked his way down through the branches of Lookout Tree and he wondered how he was going to explain this to the others. He had no idea how to fulfill his teacher's latest request of him. *"Trust your Far-vision, it will guide you"*, The Eldest One had said. Well, he was about to find out if that was true.

When he reached the lowest branch of the tree he sat for a moment and watched his People yelling and screaming at each other. He saw the anger and fear in the faces of the Young Ones. He saw their confusion. He began to look at them with his Far-vision. He wasn't sure what he was looking for, just something that would give him an idea on how to help his People. Suddenly he found himself shouting louder than he thought he could possibly shout "Stop this, stop this now".

Amazingly, they did. He waited until he had everyone's attention and he said in the same tone of voice that The Eldest One might have used "Your Home is not to be a place for fighting and hurting each other. Together, we must create Peace again. Together, we must learn to live without the help of The Eldest One."

He stopped to look into their faces. His legs were shaking, but his voice remained strong. He wasn't sure where the words were coming from but he knew that they were good words because his People were listening to him. "Tonight, we sleep and tomorrow we will begin to live Peace... and we will use our Far-vision to do it."

As they began to quietly move away to their sleeping places, he found himself thinking about The Eldest One's last words, "empower them". How was he going to do that when he wasn't even sure what it meant? He was going to have to trust his Far-vision a lot.

CHAPTER NINE

Additional Support

Quick Reference Sheets

The Weiss Transformation Processes

The Basic Process

Support: Trusted Support Being or
5th Dimensional Soul Aspect or
7th Dimensional Soul Aspect or
12th Dimensional Soul Aspect.

Purpose: To discharge stored negative emotions
To discharge stored negative memories
To replace negative belief systems with Soul Perspective.
To create new perspectives in the body.

Process: Breathe Support Being or Soul Aspect into body.
Focus on issue or memory.
Allow Support Being or Soul Aspect to also experience issue or memory.
Open to Higher Perspective
Repeat until sense of completion.

Frequency of Use: Process can be done as a form of meditation once or twice a day.

Additional: Process can be used in a modified form by breathing Support Being or Soul Aspect directly into any negative reaction experienced at any time.

Frequent and ongoing use of the modified form is highly recommended.

The Time Process

First Application

Support: 5th Dimensional Soul Aspect and
Future Self one-year-from-now or
Future Self three-year-from-now.

Purpose: To acquire Future Perspective on current issues.

Process: Breathe 5th Dimensional Soul Aspect into body.
Focus on Future Self standing beside you.
Allow Future Self to also experience issue.
Open to Future Perspective.
Repeat until sense of completion.

Frequency of Use: Process can be done as a form of meditation once or twice a day.

Additional: Process is not to be used to discern future events. It is designed to be a tool for creating insight and peace with current problems or situations.

The Time Process

Second Application

Support: 5th Dimensional Soul Aspect and
Future Self one-year-from-now or
Future Self three-years-from-now.

Purpose: To change negative belief systems developed during childhood.
To create self-empowerment and self-love.

Process: Breathe 5th Dimensional Soul Aspect into body.
Focus on Future Self standing beside you.
Focus on sleeping Past Self immediately after

negative childhood experience.

With Future Self project positive perspectives to Past Self.

Identify and focus on Past Self's Guardian Being.

Focus on Guardian Being's love and support of Past Self.

Return focus to now and open to Future Perspective.

Frequency of Use: Process can be done as a form of meditation once a day.

Additional: None

The DNA Process

First Application

Support: 5th Dimensional Soul Aspect and
7th Dimensional Soul Aspect.

Purpose: To neutralize limiting genetic Primate Survival information.

Process: Breathe 5th Dimensional Soul Aspect into body.
Breathe 7th Dimensional Soul Aspect into body.
Focus on DNA (with eyes open and using left hand, into the bones, into the.cells, into the DNA).
Focus on Soul's stream of consciousness or light flowing into hand/bones/cells/DNA.
Monitor streams progress through the body while maintaining focus on hand (etc.)
Repeat monitoring and maintaining focus until sense of completion.
Close hands and open to Soul Perspective.

Frequency of Use: Process can be done as a form of meditation once or twice a week.

Additional: The Soul is responsible for identifying which genetic coding no longer serves you and it is the Soul's energy used to create the changes in your DNA for you. Your contribution is in creating and maintaining the bridge between your Soul and your body. Your desire and willingness to do this allows the Soul to intervene in such a powerful way on your behalf.

The DNA Process

Second Application

Support: 5th Dimensional Soul Aspect and
7th Dimensional Soul Aspect and
12th Dimensional Soul Aspect.

Purpose: To activate evolutionary information in the Divine DNA.

Process: Breathe 5th Dimensional Soul Aspect into body.
Breathe 7th Dimensional Soul Aspect into body.
Breathe 12th Dimensional Soul Aspect into body.
Focus on DNA (with eyes open and using left hand, into the bones, into the cells, into the DNA).
Focus on Soul's stream of consciousness or light flowing into hand/bones/cells/DNA.
Monitor stream's progress through the body while maintaining focus on hand (etc.)
Repeat monitoring and maintaining focus until sense of completion.
Close hands and open to Soul Perspective.

Frequency of Use: Process can be done as a form of meditation once or twice a week.

Process should not be done on the same day as DNA Process – First Application.

Additional: The Soul is responsible for identifying the Divine DNA and it is the Soul's energy which is used to create the changes in your DNA for you. Your contribution is in creating and maintaining the bridge between your Soul and your body. Your desire and willingness to do this allows the Soul to intervene in such a powerful way on your behalf.

Soul's Dimensional Delineation

3rd Dimensional Reality

Form : Experienced as solid.
Experienced as separate from other forms.

Perspective: Separate from Source.
Death as the end of Self.
Reality of Duality resulting in Judgment of self and others.
Primary influence is body's Primate Perspective of Survival (avoidance of death) resulting in Fear and other negative emotions.
Secondary influence is higher dimensional Soul Aspect's Perspectives resulting in Love and other positive emotions.

Purpose: To provide Soul with the experience of this dimensional reality.

Use In Weiss Transformation Processes: Is the recipient of the effects of the Processes when changing the body's Primate Perspective is desired.

Additional: Our species is currently working to replace the Primary influence with that of the Secondary influence.

4th Dimensional Reality

Form: Experienced as solid.

Experienced as separate from other forms.

Perspective: Can reflect that of the 3rd dimensional form.

Purpose: To provide Soul with the experience of this dimensional reality.

To provide higher dimensional Soul Aspects with access to the 3rd dimensional form.

Use In Weiss Transformational Processes: None.

Additional: This form can be used by the 3rd dimensional mind for 4th dimensional travel (out-of-body, near death and after-death experiences).

5th Dimensional Reality

Form: Experienced as a light form.

Experienced as connected to but separate from other forms.

Perspective: Connected to the Source.

Is aware of the concept of Death.

Is aware of the concept of Duality.

Primary influence is its awareness of The Source in all things resulting in Love.

Is aware of the purpose for all experience, resulting in Non-judgment.

Purpose: To provide Soul with the experience of this dimensional reality.

To provide higher dimensional Soul Aspects with access to the 3rd dimensional form.

Use In Weiss Transformational Processes: Provides the 3rd dimensional form with the Perspective of Non-judgment and Unconditional Love.

Used in all of the Weiss Transformational Processes.

Additional: This is the Soul Aspect used most frequently in the modified version of the Basic Process.

7th Dimensional Reality

Form :   Experienced as a light form .
Experienced as connected to but separate from other forms.

Perspective: Connected to the Source.
Primary influence is its awareness of The Source in all things resulting in Love.
Is aware of the necessity of all experience, resulting in Appreciation and profound Peace.

Purpose: To provide Soul with the experience of this dimensional reality.
To provide higher dimensional Soul Aspects with access to the lower dimensional forms.

Use In Weiss Transformational Processes: Provides the 3rd dimensional form with the Perspective of Higher Purpose.
Basic Process and DNA Process.

Additional: None.

12th Dimensional Reality

Form: Experienced as a light form.
Experienced as having a higher connection with other individualized forms.

Perspective: As a flow of Source's consciousness.
Primary influence is its awareness of Oneness-with-all resulting in Love
Is aware of the Collective Intention for all

Experience, resulting in Appreciation and profound Peace.

Purpose: To provide Soul with the experience of this dimensional reality.

To provide higher dimensional Soul Aspects with access to the lower dimensional forms.

Use In Weiss Transformational Processes: Provides the 3rd dimensional form with the Perspectives of Acceptance and Appreciation for all experiences.

Provides the 3rd dimensional form with the Perspective of Gratitude and Joy.

Basic Process and DNA Process.

Additional: Is the primary influence in the Second Application of the DNA Process.

Is often referred to as the Christ or Buddhic level in that these Beings achieved this level of perspective in their 3rd dimensional bodies while on Earth.

Questions most frequently asked

Q. How do I know when to use the Time Process instead of the Basic Process?

A. You would use the Second Application of The Time Process when you're wanting to eliminate a specific belief system adopted in your childhood that was created as a result of trauma or a particularly negative experience. For instance, inappropriate sexual behavior on the part of an adult or older sibling would result in a number of negative beliefs about yourself and others. Continually going back and working with the child in the dream state would support the child in "re-thinking" the experience. This, of course, would quickly eliminate any resentment, fear or any of the other negative emotional responses that existed before you started using The

Process. Another side effect would be less self-judgment and more inner-strength.

Q. How do I know if I'm doing The Processes correctly?

A. If you are experiencing a sense of peace at the end of the session, then you are doing The Process correctly. If you are still feeling tense or as though there's more, then allow your Support Being or Soul Aspect to feel that with you. This will enable you to continue The Process until you do feel a sense of peace.

Q. What if I can't see anything?

A. Some people are very visual, but being visual isn't what these Processes are about. It's more important to focus on how you "feel" about a particular memory or belief. In fact, it can actually be easier to do The Processes if you can't see anything because you won't run the risk of being distracted by the visuals.

Q. What if I only believe in allowing Christ to work with me?

A. There are many people who would prefer working only with one Higher Being or another. This is absolutely all right. When we use the words "Support Being" or "Soul Aspect" or "Dimensional Soul Aspect", you may substitute Christ. When doing the Time Process, you would substitute Christ for the 5th Dimensional Soul Aspect so when you begin working with your Future Self, Christ will be available to ensure that only Truth and Healing happen for you.

The overall purpose of these Processes is to create the availability of a non-judgmental and loving perspective for your body and Christ would certainly do that for you.

Q. I've tried to do The Basic Process many times but I just can't feel anything. What should I do?

Q. What does it feel like when you can't do The Process?

A. It feels frustrating and blocked.

A. Allow your Soul to feel that with you and you're doing The Process.

Q. Are there some people for whom these processes just won't work?

A. Yes. These Processes cannot work for anyone who does not have the Soul intention to create or allow a lessening of the negativity in the body. This can be the result of the over-all life purpose or it may just be a matter of timing. If it is a matter of timing, then the person may find that The Processes will work in 6 months or in 6 years. It really does depend on what you are intending to do with your life at this time. If healing or if a shift in your body's consciousness is important to you, then these Processes will work.

Q. Sometimes when I try to do the Basic Process everything goes dark and I become afraid and stop the process. What's happening? Am I just blocking?

Q. What Support Being or Soul Aspect are you using when you do The Process?

A. My Angel.

Q. Have you allowed your Angel to experience the darkness with you?

A. No, as soon as I become afraid I stop the process.

Q. Would you like to eliminate this fear for yourself or are you happy to keep it?

A. I would like to eliminate it. I think it's somehow keeping me from making some important changes in my life.

Q. Do you trust that your Angel has more power than the darkness?

A. I'm not sure.

Q. Who or what are you sure would absolutely have more power than the darkness?

A. Archangel Michael is more powerful than the darkness and I've been thinking about using him to help me.

A. Then the next time you do The Process, let Michael work with you. My sense is that this darkness is actually something you remember from your childhood, so no matter what you see or remember happening, you keep Michael in your body feeling everything with you. And. if it is a childhood memory, it's very important to see Michael in the child's body too. This way you can begin to recreate what happened for yourself as well as eliminating the memory of darkness.

Q. I'm beginning to feel sick in my stomach.

A. That's your body's fear response. Breathe Archangel Michael into your body now and let him feel that with you. Take your time.

A. I feel better now. I'll do the process as soon as I get home.

CONCEPTS, TERMS AND DEFINITIONS
(As They Are Used In This Work)

ABSOLUTE (The) See **GOD**
ALLNESS (The)   See **GOD**
ANGELS
➢ Individualized expressions of the Creator who have never experienced the reality of duality.
➢ A constant source of non-judgment and love.
Note: Angelic Beings comprehend humans in their absolute Truth (Soulness). They exist in a constant state of truth and unconditional love, and support us in experiencing that for ourselves. Due to their non-judgmental perspective, angels sometimes function as the Trusted Support Being in The Basic Process .
ASCENSION
➢ The result of raising the frequency of the physical body to the point of no longer being visible in this dimension

153

Note: This can be accomplished by replacing low frequency thoughts, emotions or belief systems held in the body's cells and sub-conscious with the higher frequency Soul Perspective. This can be a side effect of the long term use of the WTP's.

CREATOR

➤ That aspect of God responsible for bringing the idea of Creation into existence.

DIMENSION

➤ A delineation of Creation based on a particular set of frequencies of light and/or sound.

➤ A delineation of Creation based on a predominate Soul perspective or reality.

Note: In this work, Soul is seen as a multi-dimensional phenomenon, in that it is a flow of consciousness existing in every possible perspective or reality.

DIVINE DNA

➤ Genetic material coded with information relating to the physical body's evolving nature.

Note: Allowing the Soul to focus a stream of it's intention and consciousness into specific bits of evolutionary coding allows the human body to evolve more quickly into the New Human that it was designed to become.

DUALITY

➤ The concept of opposites.

➤ A predominant reality in the 3rd dimension.

FLYING

➤ Living a Higher Dimensional Reality.

➤ The ability to live beyond the body's Primate Survival Perspective.

➤ The ability to experience life with the Soul's perspective

FUTURE SELF

➤ "You" as you exist in the Future.

Note: The primary Support Being used in WTP Two – The Time Process

GOD

➢ The mind and creative force behind all Creation.

➢ The essence of everything in Creation.

Note: Also referred to as The Source, The Allness, The Absolute.

GUARDIAN BEING

➢ Any Higher Being working full-time with the individual in the capacity of support and ongoing source of Love.

HIGHER ASPECT See **SOUL**

HIGHER BEINGS

➢ Non-physical entities exhibiting and/or sharing the higher dimensional perspectives of Love and non-judgment.

Note: In this work we are referring primarily to Ascended Masters and Angelic Beings.

HIGHER PERSPECTIVE

➢ The Soul's non-survival perspective.

HIGHER POWER See **GOD** or **SOUL**

HIGHER SELF See **SOUL**

IMAGINATION

➢ An aspect of the mind used by the individual for creativity.

➢ An aspect of the mind used by the sub-conscious for emotional release.

➢ An aspect of the mind used by the Soul to introduce new ideas, concepts and perspectives.

LOVE

➢ The honest appreciation for the essence of another.

➢ The honest appreciation for the presence of another in your life.

MONKEY

➢ Refers to the body's Primate Survival Perspective that currently dominates the human experience on Earth.

PROCESS

➢ The act of focusing on a particular negativity while including the higher perspective of Soul in order to eliminate the negativity.

SHIFT IN CONSCIOUSNESS

➤ Changing the body's primary perspective of survival and fear to that of the Soul's perspective of Love and Oneness.

SOUL

➤ A flow of consciousness from God extending through the many dimensions of Creation.

➤ The consciousness animating our human forms.

➤ Our connection with our Source.

Note: This is the main source of higher perspective used in the WTP's.

SOUL ASPECT

➤ A single dimensional expression of the Soul.

SOURCE (The) See GOD

SUPPORT BEING

➤ Non-physical entities who exhibit and share their higher dimensional realities in order to support the individual in creating a healing or shift in perspective. See also **ANGELS** and **HIGHER BEINGS.**

WEISS TRANSFORMATION PROCESSES

➤ Techniques for systematically replacing negative emotions, beliefs and paradigms with the higher perspectives of the Soul.

Note: These techniques work on both the cellular and genetic levels.

WINGS

➤ Belief systems allowing us to live the Soul's non-survival perspective.

THE STORY

Part Five

If Only They Had Wings

If only They had Wings

*H*e stands at the edge of the jungle that is his Home. He looks out into the Open Space. He is aware of the Four-Leggeds that are moving there but they are not a threat. Almost everyone uses their Far-vision now so Four-Leggeds no longer have an opportunity to make meals of his People. Life in his Home was very peaceful.

He is The Oldest Of The Elders now and he comes often here to the Edge to think and to use his Far-vision. A small rustle of leaves behind him tells him he's not alone. He turns to see three small faces peering out from the bushes. They are Young Ones and their eyes are bright with curiosity. He knows they want to join him at the Edge but they are not sure they should be disturbing him. He speaks to them. "You don't have to be afraid. They stare at him but won't come near. Except one, who slowly comes to stand beside him.

He waited, giving the Young One a chance to relax and

then asked, "What do you see?"

"I see grass and sky" the little one replied bravely. "Use your Far-vision, Young One", he prompted. After a few moments the Young One began to speak excitedly, "I see Four-Leggeds, but they aren't coming this way. I see the place where they come from in a place made of large rocks and I see.... I see Trees!!. There's another Place of Trees, but I think that it's very, very far away. There are People like us living there, but I don't think they use their Far-vision because they are still afraid of the Four-Leggeds. Can this be true, can this be true?" The Young One was hopping around excitedly waiting for him to explain. He looked at the Young One for a very long time. This little one was going to be different. It would be a good idea if he worked with him, otherwise his Greater Far-vision was going to get him into trouble.

When he realized that the Young One was about to run back into the bushes with embarrassment and fear, he said, "Young One, you must trust your Greater Far-vision. It serves you well. Be in Peace with what you see. But don't expect everyone to see or understand what you see. That will take some time." With this, he motioned for all three Young Ones to leave him. "Return now to the others", he said.

He needed to think about this new development for his People. He heard another sound behind him and thinking that it was the Young Ones again, sighed and turned to send them back into their Home. As he turned, however, he saw The Eldest One sitting there watching him. No matter how often this had occurred over the years, he still found it very unsettling. How long ago had The Eldest One been Covered Up? He couldn't remember anymore.

The Eldest One smiled and began to speak. "That Young One reminds me of you so long ago. And I remember thinking the very same thing as I spoke to you that first day. You are going to have to work with him or he will upset the People with his Greater Far-vision." The Eldest One's face turned serious as he continued, "Show him how to teach and empower the others, as you have done. He will continue what we started. He will show them how to Fly." When The Eldest One had finished speaking, he did what he always did, he disappeared.

*This was the first time anyone else had ever spoken about the things that he had seen in his own Looking. He knew there was another Place Of Trees and that it was very, very far away. He knew that another People lived there. Now a Young One had seen too and wouldn't be able to keep the information to himself. This **was** going to be a new development for his People.*

He had just begun to use his Far-vision to help him to decide what he must do to help his People be in Peace with the new development when he heard a loud commotion somewhere behind him in his Home. He moved as quickly as his not-so-young body would allow and found his People in a frenzy. For the first time in a very long time, they were running around in circles and screaming at each other. The Young One with the Greater Far-vision was in the center of all the screaming so understanding the cause of the frenzy wasn't difficult.

He stood unobserved for awhile watching to see if they would be able to resolve this for themselves. Instead, the screaming and chaos became even worse. He could see the fear and anger on their faces as they pointed at the Young One screaming that he mustn't say such things. "There can't be others, we are the only People, we are the only People" they yelled repeatedly at the Young One crouching in their center.

When the Young One looked as though he might be in danger he, the Oldest of The Elders, stepped forward and shouted loud enough to be heard by all, "Stop this, stop this now". He was always amazed and grateful that this worked. He waited in the silence that followed until he had everyone's attention and he began to speak slowly so that everyone would understand the importance of his words. "You must not harm this Young One for sharing his Greater Far-vision. You must develop your own Greater Far-vision to confirm this new information and to understand what it means to us." Then he spoke to the Young One. "You must teach them to use their Greater Far-vision, Young Elder. You must teach them what you know. We must have Peace again in our home". He left them in their silence and went back to The Edge to continue with his Looking.

The following months were a mixture of revelation and insanity. Those who would allow themselves to learn and use their Greater Far-vision were in complete acceptance of the fact that their Home wasn't the only Home and that The World didn't end where the Open Space met the Sky. They found the idea exciting and wanted to know what else might exist beyond that place. The newest Young Teaching Elder, who's Greater Far-vision had started the uproar, found himself nearly overwhelmed with the demand for him to "teach them what you know" and he quickly learned to show other Teaching Elders how to help him.

Those of his People who weren't able to open to the idea of other People, no matter how far away, remained very agitated and started quarrels with the others. Often as he moved through the trees he found them arguing loudly about the validity of the information. The other disturbing subject to many was the question as to whether or not these other People might somehow be a threat to them. "What if the other People also developed Far-vision, could they somehow make their way into our Home and hurt us."

For the first time ever, his People were divided against each other. He spent much of his time at The Edge hoping that

The Eldest One would suddenly show up behind him to give him advice. Only Young Ones joined him at The Edge wanting to share what they saw in their Looking. He would listen to them for a little while before sending them back to their Teaching Elders or mothers. He needed time alone to decide what he was going to do to help heal his People. Whenever he attempted to use his Far-vision to get an answer, he was reminded of The Eldest One's last words to him "He will show them how to Fly".

He was thinking about what this might mean as he made his way back into his Home to calm the louder quarrels that had begun happening more and more frequently. As he moved through the trees, he noticed a small group of Young Elders sitting quietly with the Young Teaching Elder in their midst. They all had their eyes closed. He waited until they began to move and speak before going over to them. "What were you doing Young Elder?" he asked and he wasn't at all surprised when he heard the answer, "I was teaching them how to Fly".

The explanation that followed, however, was very

surprising. "Each time that I used my Greater Far-vision to look into the Home of the other People", the Young Elder began, "I realized that I could see things there more and more clearly. I also realized that it was as if I could be there and here at the same time. It's not as though I had two bodies, exactly, only that I could be in two places".

He noticed the Young Elder hesitating, unsure if he should say more, so he nodded and gestured for him to continue. "I was thinking about the fear that some of our People have about the other People somehow hurting us", the Young Elder said slowly, "and I thought... I thought that it might be helpful if we could see what was in the hearts of the other People". I thought that if some of us could Fly over there, we could see what kind of People they are. I thought we could see if any of them even know how to use Far-vision", the young one finished in a rush. "And what did you find", the Oldest of The Elders asked trying to keep his voice steady. The Young Elder waited a long moment before answering, "They are very much as we are. They live, eat, sleep and have The Covering Up just as we do. I do not think that they would harm us even if they could come so far to our Home". There was another long pause and then, "They do not have Far-vision... yet."

He waited for the Young Elder to gather his courage before asking him to continue. He was not prepared for what came next. "Once when I was not just Looking but also Flying, I realized that one of their Young Ones could see me. He was standing next to a tree and he was looking right at me. I smiled at him and he smiled back. I have visited him many times and others of his People are beginning to notice what he is doing. When he tries to explain to them they become upset with him. They would hurt him except that their Eldest One stops them. He has seen me too."

This was more than he was ready to hear and he knew that he was going to have to think very carefully about what to do about this newest development that the Young Elder had created. Yes, he was going to have to work closely with that one. He instructed the Young Teaching Elder to share what he had learned about the other People but to wait before he gave any more lessons in Flying.

If the People in **his** Home were having a difficult time

with all of the changes, how would it be for the People in the other Home? They didn't know how to use their Far-vision to help them to be at Peace. If only they had their wings.

He made his way back to The Edge. He needed to think about this. He must talk with The Eldest One. He must. When he got to The Edge, he was surprised to see The Eldest One waiting for him. He was so happy that he nearly shouted, "I've been needing to talk to you". His teacher didn't answer right away and turned again to look out into the Open Space. Finally he said, "I'm not The Eldest One that you need to talk to. You must Fly to the other Home and speak with their Eldest One". As his teacher began to disappear, he heard him say, "Teach him what you know."

CHAPTER TEN

Can Monkeys Be Angels? Or What Happens When The Sky Is No Longer The Limit?

As we begin to adopt the Soul's Perspective in our lives, we find that just about everything changes. The Soul's Perspective of non-judgment reduces the body's fear, which in turn reduces its stress and tension. The Perspective of unconditional love changes the quality of every relationship. Turning Self-judgment into Self-acceptance creates a peaceful way of dealing with new situations and people. It can also create a new relationship with your body.

The most striking of changes, however, is the quiet acceptance of the negativity that is in or around others. It will be seen as a quiet peace that becomes your contribution to every negative situation. It will also be seen as a quiet power.

You will become very aware of the flow of things in your life; the synchronicity of it all. You will begin to truly appreciate each contributing factor whether it's a situation or a person. The uniqueness of anyone you know or encounter becomes increasingly apparent and a deep appreciation for those who love you frequently takes you by surprise.

You will do nothing to make others feel badly about themselves but you won't be capable of lying to them either.

You will always be looking for the higher reason for things and you will always strive to stay in keeping with the greater Truth. You will allow Higher Purpose to guide you and you will be grateful for the opportunity to walk this Earth.

And.... you will be noticed. You will be questioned about your perspectives and you will allow the questioner's Soul to help you form your answer into something that will be understood. You will be challenged about your beliefs and you will allow your inner peace to flow through the exchange. You will be doubted and you will release the doubter to their own Soul's plan. You will be honored as a wise one and you will remember that we are all, in essence, the same precious expression of Life. Above all, you will know that there is a Purpose for everything and a Time for everything and you will be at absolute peace with and appreciation of both.

And.... you will be asked to Teach them. You will be asked to Heal them. You will be asked to work miracles in their lives. You will say "yes" to some and you will say "no" to others. Your answers will always be based on the combined answer that will come from your Soul and theirs. Every interaction you have with another will, in some way, work to empower them; to remind them that they also have an inner source of knowledge. You will not carry them or be responsible for them. You will constantly remind them that their own Higher Power is in charge of what happens in their life. One of your greatest gifts to them will be your ability to focus on their Higher Power.

And... you will be misunderstood. You may even be feared. You will always be surprised when it happens and you will always be in peace with it because you understand. You will understand how human nature can sometimes be. You will also understand that you are ultimately in charge of what happens to you in your life and that the anger or fear of another has no real power to hurt you. You will confuse them with your ability to love them in spite of their behavior towards you. Some of them will be moved to their own healing by your ability to do this.

And.... you won't be capable of acting normal. Whether it's your choices in food, entertainment or conversational topics, you will have a perspective that is different from most of those around you. You will look around at the world's insanity and see it as a form of healing. You will look around at the world's negativity and see it as being temporary. You will find yourself having long and meaningful conversations with things like trees and dolphins. You won't mind if others hear you.

The entire planet will become your home and the beings who move about her surface will seem as brothers and sisters. Life will become an incredible opportunity for which you are extremely grateful. You will be also be extremely grateful for the increasing number of individuals who are doing exactly the same thing with their lives. You will admire their courage and applaud their efforts for you understand all too well.

You will begin to awaken to an even greater understanding of the contribution that you are making to your Planet and to your species. You will begin to awaken to the contribution that your Planet and your species is making to the universe. You will begin to be aware of others in the universe who are also making a contribution to your Planet and your species.

You will continue to expand your ability to accept and integrate the universal aspects of what your Soul knows. You will do this without losing any of your humanity. You will do this without losing any of your friends. You will do this without losing your sense of humor.

You will laugh. You will cry. You will love. And.... you will *fly*.

THE STORY

Part Six

The Conclusion

The Conclusion

*H*e wanted to go up into the highest branches of Lookout Tree just once more but his body wasn't capable of the climb. He wanted to see his Home from up high. He wanted to see it all one more time before he left his body. He knew that it was time. He was very tired and knew that he had done all that he could do with one life.

His People were content and at Peace. The People in the Homes that they had discovered through their Greater Far-vision had become a source of companionship and information. Over the years, his People had learned a lot about what some of the others called The Planet. Each new Home that they visited in their Flying offered a different piece of information about this great collection of Homes.

There had been some challenges too. They had to learn how to present themselves to the People in each new Home in a way that didn't create fear and chaos. They learned to wait until they were noticed, and to go slowly with their explanations of who they were and where they were from. They also learned that *it was easier if only one or two of them went Flying into a newly discovered Home, rather than overwhelming the People with large numbers of them suddenly showing up in their midst.*

Yes, it had been quite an education and quite a life. He wondered how his old teacher felt about it all. He hadn't seen him since the day he went to meet The Eldest One in the other Home that they had first discovered. He missed his teacher.

He walked among his People one last time. They knew that he would be going and everyone was very quiet. Some of them had even begun gathering things to use in his Covering Up. He was glad that they knew. It gave him a chance to say good-bye.

When he felt complete, he returned to the base of Lookout Tree where his Looking had first begun. How he wished that he could make his way back up to the top. Suddenly, he was.

He thought at first that it was his Far-vision that gave him the sense of being back up there, but no, he was actually sitting in the highest branches. "Ah, I've left my body", he said to his old teacher who was sitting right beside him. They sat in silence for a time as he looked out over his Home. **His** Home, spreading out until it touched the sky in three directions. "My Home", he whispered. "No", his Teacher said beside him. "**This** is your Home". What he saw next was beyond his comprehension. It was a round thing floating in a darkness and he couldn't understand what he was seeing.

"Use your Far-vision" he heard his Teacher's voice say. When he did, he realized that he was seeing all the Homes spread out over the round thing. This must be The Planet. As he continued his Looking, he realized that this was not the only round thing with Homes on it. He realized that there were many Planets with Homes out in the darkness. That means that there must be other People out there as well.

This was an exciting idea and he felt as he did in his younger days when he first learned that he had Far-vision. "Can we Fly to those Planets too?" he asked his Teacher. "Yes", was the reply. "Then we'll return to your Home and..."

"I know, I know", he said interrupting. "I'll teach them what I know".

Thanks

On Behalf of myself and all the Beings who worked with me to create this, I say thank you for allowing us to be of service. As you are the Creator's Light, we do acknowledge you. May you be in Peace.